EMMA MAXWELL

LLC for Beginners Made Easy

This book was professionally typeset on Reedsy.
Find out more at reedsy.com

Contents

Introduction

When my son was born, I found myself at a crossroads. As a CPA qualified accountant, I had spent years honing my skills, but I realized I had never truly grasped the financial basics that could make or break my family's future. It was a humbling moment, but it ignited a fire within me to embark on a journey of learning and growth.

As I navigated the complexities of setting up my own business, I encountered countless challenges and made my fair share of mistakes. But with each setback, I gained invaluable insights that I knew could help others in similar situations. That's why I decided to write this book—to share my hard-earned knowledge and provide a clear, accessible guide for anyone looking to start their own Limited Liability Company (LLC).

Whether you're a seasoned business person, a sole trader, a freelancer, or a publisher, this book is designed to demystify the process of setting up an LLC. I understand the unique challenges you face and the aspirations you hold dear. My goal is to break down complex concepts into manageable steps, empowering you to make informed decisions about your business structure.

Throughout these pages, you'll discover the advantages and disadvantages of forming an LLC, learn how it differs from other business structures, and gain a clear understanding of the ongoing costs associated with maintaining an LLC. I'll guide you through the step-by-step process of formation, help you navigate tax implications, and provide practical tips to ensure your LLC runs smoothly.

So, what will you gain from this book? Here are the key takeaways:

- The benefits of forming an LLC
- The differences between an LLC and other structures

- Choosing a Business Name
- Filing your Articles of Association
- LLC bookkeeping and tax strategies
- Expanding and growing within your LLC
- Industry-specific case studies

But this book is more than just theoretical advice. Throughout this book, I've included real-life examples from my own journey, as well as actionable strategies to help you apply what you learn. By the end of this guide, you'll have the confidence and clarity you need to embark on your entrepreneurial journey with your LLC.

The book is structured logically, starting with the basics and moving on to more advanced topics. Here's a brief overview of the chapters;

1. Understanding LLC Basics
2. Step-by-Step Guide to LLC Formation
3. Financial and Tax Strategies for LLCs
4. Legal Compliance and Maintenance
5. Expanding and Scaling your LLC
6. Advanced LLC Strategies and Considerations
7. Industry-Specific Guidance for LLCs
8. Enhancing your LLC Journey

As you read, I encourage you to take notes, mark sections for further research, and actively apply the lessons to your own business endeavors. This book is designed to be an interactive experience, one that empowers you to take control of your financial future.

Each chapter will end with specific, actionable steps you can take to improve your financial situation right away. You'll have a clear path to follow, making it easier to take control of your LLC journey.

Remember, understanding and applying financial knowledge has the power to transform your life and your business. By taking the time to educate yourself and make informed decisions, you're setting yourself up for success. So let's dive in together and unlock the potential of your LLC.

Chapter 1

Understanding LLC Basics

Starting a business can feel like standing at the edge of a vast, unexplored territory. There's excitement, but also a fair share of uncertainty. You might have a brilliant idea or a passion you're ready to transform into a venture, but the thought of navigating legal structures can seem daunting. I remember a conversation I had with a fellow freelancer who had just made the leap from a sole proprietorship to an LLC. She described the peace of mind she felt knowing her personal assets were shielded from business liabilities. Her story embodies the essence of what an LLC offers—protection, flexibility, and a sense of security in the entrepreneurial journey.

1.1 Defining an LLC – What It Means for Your Business

An LLC, or Limited Liability Company, is a unique business structure that offers the best of both worlds. It combines the personal liability protection of a corporation with the tax efficiencies and operational flexibility of a partnership. This hybrid nature makes it an appealing choice for many entrepreneurs, especially those looking to protect their personal assets from potential business risks. In an LLC, your personal wealth is generally insulated from business debts and liabilities, meaning creditors can't seize your house or savings account if your business encounters financial trouble. This limited liability protection is one of the most compelling reasons to consider forming an LLC.

Pass-through taxation is another significant advantage. Unlike a corporation, which is taxed at the corporate level, an LLC allows profits to pass through directly to its owners, meaning you'll report your LLC's income on your personal tax return. This can simplify your tax situation and potentially save you from the double taxation that corporations face. Yet, an LLC is more than just a tax-friendly entity; it offers unmatched operational flexibility. Whether you're a one-person operation or have multiple partners, an LLC can be tailored to fit your specific needs. You can structure your business management in a way that aligns with your goals, deciding how profits are distributed, how decisions are made, and who takes on specific roles within the company.

Understanding the terminology associated with LLCs is crucial for navigating this structure effectively. At the core, you'll encounter terms like "member" and "manager." Members are the owners of the LLC, akin to shareholders in a corporation. They hold stakes in the business and have a say in its operations. Managers, on the other hand, are responsible for running the day-to-day activities, and in some cases, a member can also serve as a manager. Then, there are the "Articles of Organization," a fundamental document you'll need to file with your state to officially form your LLC. This document outlines essential details like the LLC's name, address, and the names of its members or managers, serving as the legal foundation of your business.

What makes an LLC particularly appealing is its hybrid nature, blending elements of both corporations and partnerships. From corporations, it borrows the concept of shielding personal assets from business liabilities, offering corporate-style protection. Yet, unlike a corporation, it doesn't impose the same level of administrative burdens or paperwork. From partnerships, an LLC takes the taxation model, allowing income to flow through to its members without facing corporate taxes. This means you enjoy the benefits of partnership-style taxation without sacrificing the liability protection a corporation provides.

Administratively, maintaining an LLC is relatively straightforward, but there are a few key requirements to keep in mind. You'll need to appoint a registered agent, who acts as your business's official contact for receiving legal documents. This person or entity must have a physical address in the state where your LLC operates. Additionally, while not always legally required, having an Operating Agreement is highly recommended. This internal document outlines the ownership and management structure of your LLC, detailing the roles and responsibilities of each member, the division of profits, and procedures for adding or removing members. It can prevent disputes and ensure everyone is on the same page, providing a clear road map for how your business will function.

As you consider forming an LLC, remember that this structure offers flexibility and control, allowing you to craft a business that fits your vision and lifestyle. Whether you're a freelancer protecting your creative work or a small business owner expanding operations, an LLC provides a robust framework for growth and security.

1.2 Key Benefits of Forming an LLC

When considering the formation of an LLC, one of the most compelling reasons lies in its robust liability protection. Imagine you've poured your heart, soul, and savings into your business, only to face a lawsuit that threatens your personal assets. With an LLC, this nightmare scenario is largely mitigated. The structure of an LLC acts as a shield, protecting your personal wealth— your home, savings, and other valuables —from being targeted in the event of a business-related lawsuit. This protection is not just theoretical; it's a legal framework that has helped countless entrepreneurs sleep easier at night, knowing their personal finances remain secure. This separation between personal and business liabilities distinguishes LLCs as a preferred choice for those who wish to safeguard personal assets while taking calculated business risks.

The tax advantages of an LLC are equally noteworthy, offering a level of flexibility that can be tailored to suit your specific business needs. For instance, when you operate as a single-member LLC, you can enjoy the simplicity of pass-through taxation, where your business income is reported on your personal tax return, avoiding the double taxation faced by corporations. This means you're not taxed twice—once at the corporate level and again on your personal income, which can result in significant tax savings. Additionally, multi-member LLCs benefit from the ability to distribute income in a manner that optimally leverages each member's tax situation. This flexibility allows you to structure your tax liabilities in a way that aligns with your financial objectives, providing a strategic advantage in managing your business finances.

Beyond liability protection and tax benefits, the operational simplicity of an LLC also stands out as a major advantage. Unlike corporations, which are often bogged down by extensive formalities and regulatory requirements, LLCs offer a streamlined approach to business management. You won't find yourself drowning in paperwork or burdened by the need to conduct formal board meetings unless you choose to. This ease of administration means you can focus more on growing your business and less on navigating bureaucratic hurdles. For many small business owners and freelancers, this simplicity translates into more time and resources to dedicate to what truly matters—developing products, serving clients, and expanding market presence.

Furthermore, forming an LLC can significantly enhance your business's credibility and professionalism in the eyes of clients and partners. In today's competitive market, perception is crucial. When potential clients see that you've taken the step to establish an LLC, it signals a level of commitment and seriousness about your business. It conveys that you're not just a fly-by-night operation, but a legitimate and stable entity. This perceived legitimacy can make a substantial difference in winning contracts, securing partnerships, and building trust with stakeholders. For example, a freelance graphic designer who transitions from a sole proprietorship to an LLC may find that clients view her services with greater respect, leading to more opportunities and higher rates.

Case Study: A Freelance Designer's Transformation

Consider the case of a freelance designer who started as a sole proprietor. Initially, her business operated on a word-of-mouth basis, sustained by personal referrals. However, as she sought to expand her client base beyond local recommendations, she encountered skepticism from potential clients unfamiliar with her work. By forming an LLC, she not only protected her personal assets but also enhanced her business's reputation. The LLC status allowed her to confidently market her services to larger corporations, leading to a significant increase in contracts and a stronger negotiating position. This transformation exemplifies how the benefits of an LLC extend beyond legal and financial realms, fostering growth through enhanced credibility and operational efficiency.

For business people, sole traders, and freelancers, the decision to form an LLC is often driven by these tangible benefits. It's not merely a legal formality, but a strategic move that supports long-term success and stability. With protection, flexibility, and professionalism at its core, an LLC provides the foundation needed to thrive in a dynamic business environment.

1.3 LLC vs. Other Business Structures – A Comparative Study

Choosing the right business structure is a pivotal decision. Many entrepreneurs start with sole proprietorships due to their simplicity and low costs. It's the natural choice for those who want to dip their toes into the business world without formalities. However, this simplicity comes with significant drawbacks. The most striking is personal liability. Sole proprietors are personally responsible for all business debts and obligations. This means that if your business accrues debt or faces litigation, your personal assets—like your home or savings—are at risk. Imagine a small bakery run as a sole proprietorship. If a customer slips and falls, the owner could face a lawsuit that threatens their personal wealth if they don't have insurance or the insurance they do have is not enough. An LLC offers a safeguard against such vulnerabilities, providing a layer of protection that can be crucial for peace of mind and financial security.

In contrast, traditional partnerships involve shared liability among partners. Each partner can be held accountable for business debts and any actions taken by the other partners. Consider a partnership between two freelance writers who decide to collaborate. If one writer makes a costly mistake, both are financially liable. This shared risk can strain relationships and complicate business operations. An LLC mitigates this by offering limited liability, ensuring that each member's personal assets are shielded from the business's liabilities. Moreover, partnerships typically flow income directly to partners, which can complicate tax matters. LLCs, however, offer flexible tax treatment, allowing members to decide how they want to be taxed, providing a strategic advantage over traditional partnerships.

Corporations stand as another option, renowned for their robust liability protection. Yet, they come with a heavy administrative burden. Corporations must conduct regular board meetings, document corporate minutes, and follow strict governance protocols. This can be overwhelming, especially for small business owners who want to focus on growth instead of paperwork. Imagine a tech startup trying to innovate while bogged down by corporate formalities. An LLC avoids these burdens, allowing business owners to concentrate on their core activities without the constant need for bureaucratic compliance. This operational freedom makes LLCs an attractive alternative for those seeking protection without the admin hassle.

When comparing LLCs to S-Corps, the differences become nuanced. An S-Corp is not a business entity but a tax designation that can be elected by corporations and LLCs meeting specific criteria. S-Corps allow for pass-through taxation, similar to LLCs, but impose restrictions. For instance, S-Corps limit the number of shareholders and require them to be U.S. citizens or residents. In contrast, LLCs offer ownership flexibility without such limitations, allowing for numerous members and diverse ownership structures. This flexibility can be crucial for businesses anticipating growth or seeking investment from foreign partners.

Moreover, an LLC provides a greater degree of operational flexibility. While S-Corps must adhere to strict shareholder and formal management requirements, LLCs can operate with more fluidity, adapting to the needs of their members. This adaptability is particularly advantageous for industries characterized by rapid change, such as technology and media. Consider a dynamic publishing house that needs to pivot quickly in response to market trends. The LLC structure supports such agility, enabling businesses to make swift decisions without the encumbrance of rigid corporate rules.

In the table below, it shows the differences between all of the ownership structures;

Business structure	Ownership	Liability	Taxes
Sole proprietorship	One person	Unlimited personal liability	Self-employment tax Personal tax
Partnerships	Two or more people	Unlimited personal liability unless structured as a limited partnership	Self-employment tax (except for limited partners) Personal tax
Limited liability company (LLC)	One or more people	Owners are not personally liable	Self-employment tax Personal tax or corporate tax
Corporation - C Corp	One or more people	Owners are not personally liable	Corporate tax
Corporation - S Corp	100 people or fewer Certain trusts and estates No partnerships, corporations, or non-resident aliens	Owners are not personally liable	Personal tax

In essence, while each business structure has its merits, the LLC often emerges as the preferred choice for those seeking a balance between protection, tax efficiency, and operational ease. Whether you're a freelancer looking to protect personal assets or a growing business navigating complex markets, the LLC offers a versatile framework for achieving your goals.

1.4 Common Misconceptions About LLCs

The concept of an LLC, while immensely beneficial, is often clouded by a series of misconceptions that can deter potential owners from embracing its full potential. A prevalent myth surrounding LLCs is the extent of liability protection they offer. Many believe that forming an LLC provides an impenetrable shield against all personal liability. While LLCs indeed protect personal assets from business debts and lawsuits, there are situations where this protection might not hold. For instance, if you personally guarantee a loan for your business, your assets could be at risk if the business defaults. Similarly, the notion of "piercing the corporate veil" is a legal concept where courts can hold members personally liable if they misuse the LLC structure, such as commingling personal and business funds or engaging in fraudulent activities. Understanding these nuances is crucial to maintaining the protective barrier that an LLC offers.

Taxation is another area ripe with confusion. A common misunderstanding is that LLCs have a default tax classification that automatically leads to tax benefits. In reality, the IRS does not tax LLCs directly. Instead, they are taxed by default as sole proprietorships or partnerships, depending on the number of members. This pass-through taxation means that the business's income is reported on the personal tax returns of its owners, potentially offering tax savings. However, an LLC can choose to be taxed as an S Corporation or C Corporation if it aligns better with their financial strategy. Misunderstanding these options can lead to poor tax planning and missed opportunities for optimization. Knowing your choices and consulting with a tax professional can ensure that your LLC's tax structure aligns with your business goals.

Another myth that often circulates is the idea that forming and maintaining an LLC is prohibitively expensive. While it's true that there are costs involved, they are generally lower than those associated with forming a corporation. The specific fees can vary widely from state to state, with some states charging as little as $50 for filing the Articles of Organization, while others might charge several hundred dollars. There are also ongoing fees, such as annual report filings or franchise taxes, but these are typically manageable within the broader scope of business expenses. The key is to budget for these costs upfront and consider them as part of the investment in your business's legitimacy and protection.

Operational complexity is another area where misconceptions abound. Many entrepreneurs shy away from LLCs, mistakenly believing that they are as cumbersome to manage as corporations. In truth, LLCs are designed to be straightforward and flexible. They have fewer formal requirements than corporations, such as the lack of mandatory board meetings and the absence of stringent record-keeping obligations. This simplicity extends to daily operations, where LLCs can be run according to the preferences of their members, without needing to adhere to rigid corporate protocols. For a freelance writer or a small e-commerce business owner, this flexibility means more time to focus on creativity and growth, rather than being bogged down by administrative minutiae.

Reflection Section: Reassessing LLC Myths

Take a moment to reflect on the myths you've encountered about LLCs. Think about how these misconceptions may have influenced your perception of forming an LLC. Consider jotting down any questions or concerns you still have about LLCs, and use this book as a resource to seek clarity. Remember, understanding the realities behind these misconceptions can empower you to make informed decisions that align with your entrepreneurial aspirations.

1.5 Evaluating if an LLC is Right for Your Business

Choosing the right structure for your business requires a clear alignment of your goals with the benefits an LLC can offer. At the forefront of your decision-making process should be your growth objectives. Consider where you envision your business in the coming years. Are you looking to expand your operations, attract investors, or perhaps scale your operations regionally or nationally? An LLC can provide the framework necessary for growth by offering a flexible structure that adapts to the complexities of scaling. This is especially beneficial for those who anticipate rapid growth and need a structure that can accommodate change without entangling them in unnecessary bureaucracy. Moreover, risk management is another crucial factor. The unique protection offered by an LLC can mitigate potential business risks, ensuring that personal assets remain secure as you navigate business uncertainties.

Industry-specific needs also play a pivotal role in determining whether an LLC is the right fit for your business. Consider the nature of your industry and the specific demands it places on business structures. For service-based industries, such as consulting or freelancing, the personal liability protection of an LLC can safeguard your personal finances against professional liability claims. This is particularly critical if your business involves rendering professional advice or services where the risk of litigation is higher. Conversely, product-based businesses, such as retail or manufacturing, might prioritize an LLC for its ability to handle inventory management and distribution logistics without compromising liability protection. The flexibility of an LLC allows you to tailor your business operations to the unique challenges and opportunities your industry presents, ensuring that your chosen structure aligns with your strategic objectives.

Financial implications are another critical consideration when evaluating the suitability of an LLC. It is essential to weigh the initial setup costs against the long-term financial benefits. Although forming an LLC can incur higher initial costs than a sole proprietorship or partnership, these expenses are often offset by the potential tax savings and liability protection an LLC provides.

Initial setup costs include state filing fees, legal fees for drafting an Operating Agreement, and potential costs for appointing a registered agent. However, these upfront investments contribute to establishing a credible and legally compliant business foundation. Furthermore, ongoing compliance expenses, such as annual report filings and franchise taxes, are manageable and can be budgeted as part of your regular business expenses. Understanding these financial responsibilities will help you make an informed decision, ensuring that the benefits of an LLC outweigh the associated costs.

A practical example might illuminate this process further. Imagine a small business owner in the tech industry, developing innovative software solutions. Her vision includes rapid expansion and attracting venture capital investments. She might find that an LLC offers the flexibility to bring in new members and distribute equity without the restrictions of other structures. Furthermore, the liability protection ensures that her personal assets remain separate from the risks associated with software development and potential intellectual property disputes. By using the decision-making framework, she can systematically evaluate her goals, assess industry needs, and weigh financial implications, ultimately making an informed decision that aligns with her growth trajectory and risk management strategies.

1.6 Real-Life Examples of Successful LLCs

Exploring real-life examples of successful LLCs across diverse industries not only illustrates the versatility of this business structure but also provides practical insights into how it can be leveraged to achieve remarkable growth and resilience. In the realm of technology startups, LLCs have become a favored choice for entrepreneurs eager to innovate without the heavy regulatory burdens of a corporation. Take the example of a small tech firm that began as a local initiative, developing niche software solutions. By forming an LLC, the founders were able to protect their personal assets while attracting investment from angel investors. Their ability to offer flexibility in ownership and quickly reinvest profits into research and development allowed them to expand their team and scale their operations significantly. This strategic growth, fueled by a combination of innovative products and a robust business structure, demonstrates how LLCs can serve as a catalyst for success in fast-paced industries.

Creative agencies, too, have found LLCs to be a perfect fit, offering a blend of protection and flexibility that aligns with their dynamic and often unpredictable nature. Consider a boutique graphic design firm that initially operated as a small partnership. By transitioning to an LLC, they were able to formalize their business model, attract high-profile clients, and collaborate with other creative professionals without the fear of personal liability. This change not only enhanced their credibility but also provided a framework for growth as they expanded their services to include digital marketing and branding. The ability to bring in new partners and share profits according to contributions rather than ownership percentages allowed the agency to adapt swiftly to market changes, ensuring its continued success in a competitive field.

Case Study: Innovation to Drive Growth

Innovation is the lifeblood of successful businesses, and LLCs provide an ideal platform for fostering creative thinking and disruptive products. A prime example can be seen in a startup that revolutionized the food delivery industry with a novel app designed to connect local farmers with urban consumers. By adopting an LLC structure, the founders enjoyed the freedom to explore unconventional business models and form strategic partnerships with local vendors. The legal protection afforded by the LLC encouraged risk-taking and experimentation, ultimately leading to a groundbreaking service that transformed the local food ecosystem. This story highlights the potential of LLCs to drive innovation, offering a fertile ground for ideas that challenge the status quo and redefine industry standards.

As you consider forming an LLC, this real-life example illustrates the diverse opportunities and advantages that this business structure can offer. Whether you're an entrepreneur in the tech world, a creative professional, or a small business owner navigating economic uncertainties, an LLC can provide the flexibility, protection, and support needed to achieve your goals. It serves as a testament to the power of strategic planning and the importance of choosing a business structure that aligns with your vision. Embrace the possibilities that an LLC can offer, and you may find that it not only protects your assets but also propels your business to new heights.

Don't move on to the next chapter without doing the following;

1. Are there any myths you wrote down in the reflection section that you need help to dispel? Write down these questions, ready for a CPA accountant or lawyer to answer when the time is right.

Chapter 2

Step-by-Step Guide to LLC Formation

The decision to form an LLC marks a significant milestone in your entrepreneurial path. It signifies a commitment to structure, to protection, and to the relentless pursuit of your business goals. But before you can dive into the formation process, it's crucial to ensure you're fully prepared for the journey ahead. As a CPA, I've learned that preparation is the cornerstone of any successful venture. Without a solid foundation, even the most promising business ideas can falter. So let's take a moment to assess your readiness and gather the necessary tools to embark on this transformative endeavor.

Assessing your readiness for LLC formation involves a thorough examination of your financial standing and an understanding of your unique business needs. Start by conducting a financial assessment. This means evaluating your current financial situation, including cash flow, existing debts, and projected income. You need a clear picture of your financial capacity to sustain the early stages of your LLC. Are you relying on personal savings, or will you need to secure additional funding? Understanding your financial landscape helps in making informed decisions about investments and expenses associated with forming an LLC. Alongside financial assessment, it's essential to pinpoint your business needs. Consider the nature of your business, the scale of operations, and your growth aspirations. This clarity will guide you in structuring your LLC to align with your vision, ensuring it meets both short-term goals and long-term objectives.

Once you've assessed your readiness, it's time to gather the necessary documentation. Proper documentation is the backbone of your LLC's formation process. Begin with personal identification, as you'll need to verify your identity in official filings. Secure any relevant business licenses and permits applicable to your industry and location. These legal requirements vary by state and industry, so it's crucial to research and obtain all necessary documentation to avoid any compliance issues down the road. Having these documents in place not only facilitates a smooth formation process but also establishes a solid foundation for legal and operational compliance.

Funding is another critical component of your LLC formation. Planning for initial funding involves exploring various financial options to ensure your business has the resources it needs to thrive. Personal savings are often the first port of call for many entrepreneurs, providing a straightforward way to finance your new venture. However, if your savings fall short, consider applying for small business loans. These loans can provide the capital needed to cover startup costs, from filing fees to operational expenses. Research different lenders, compare interest rates, and assess repayment terms to find the most suitable financing option for your LLC. Having a clear financial plan in place will help mitigate risks and set your business on a path to stability and growth.

Understanding the timeline for LLC formation is crucial for effective planning and execution. The entire process involves several stages, each with its own time frame. Start by preparing your documentation, which typically takes a few days to a week, depending on the complexity of your business and the availability of required documents. Once your paperwork is ready, the next step is filing your Articles of Organization, which officially registers your LLC with the state. The processing time for state filings varies, with some states offering expedited services for an additional fee. On average, you can expect this step to take anywhere from a week to several weeks. It's important to account for these time frames in your planning to ensure a seamless transition from conception to formation. By understanding each stage and preparing accordingly, you'll be well-equipped to navigate the LLC formation process with confidence and clarity.

Reflection Section: Assessing Your Readiness

Take a moment to reflect on your current financial and business situation. Consider writing down any questions or concerns about the LLC formation process, and use this book as a resource to seek clarity. Evaluate whether you have the necessary documentation and funding in place to proceed. This reflection will help solidify your understanding and ensure you're fully prepared for the next steps in forming your LLC.

2.1 Choosing a Business Name and Checking Availability

Choosing a business name is a creative and strategic endeavor, one that reflects the essence of your business and resonates with your target audience. It's not just a label; it's an identity that captures what your business stands for and the mission it aims to fulfill. Start by brainstorming ideas that align with your business mission. Consider what you want your name to convey. Is it a sense of innovation, reliability, or perhaps creativity? Reflecting on these attributes can help guide your brainstorming process. You want a name that is memorable, one that sticks with people after a single mention. It should be easy to pronounce and spell, ensuring that potential clients and partners can recall it effortlessly.

Once you have a shortlist of potential names, it's time to check their availability. This step is crucial to avoid legal issues down the road. You'll want to start by searching through state business name databases, which can usually be accessed online through your Secretary of State's website. These databases will show whether your desired name is already in use or if it's available. Beyond this, it's wise to perform a trademark search using tools like the United States Patent and Trademark Office's database. This ensures that your name hasn't been trademarked by another entity, which could lead to costly legal disputes. These checks are not just formalities; they are safeguards to protect your brand's uniqueness and identity.

Reserving your business name is an important step once you've ensured its availability. Many states offer an option to reserve a name for a certain period while you complete the rest of your formation process. This prevents others from registering the name during this period, giving you peace of mind. The process typically involves filling out a reservation form and paying a small fee. Check with your state's specific requirements, as the procedures and fees can vary. This reservation is a temporary hold, so it's essential to proceed with your LLC formation promptly to secure the name permanently.

In today's digital age, establishing an online presence is vital for any business. Therefore, it's wise to consider domain name availability alongside your business name. A matching domain name helps maintain consistency across your brand's online platforms, making it easier for customers to find and engage with you. Use domain registration platforms to check if your desired domain is available. If it's already taken, consider slight variations or alternative extensions like .net or .co. Registering your domain name early is a proactive step in building your business's digital foundation.

Your business name is the first impression you make on potential clients and partners. It's a representation of your values and the promise you make to your customers. As such, it deserves careful thought and consideration. By following these steps—brainstorming with intent, verifying through diligent research, reserving strategically, and securing your online presence—you lay a strong foundation for your LLC's identity.

2.2 Drafting and Filing Your Articles of Organization

The Articles of Organization is a pivotal document in the formation of your LLC. Picture it as the blueprint of your business's legal foundation, setting the stage for your entity's existence in the eyes of the state. This document essentially legitimizes your business, confirming your LLC's formation and outlining its basic structure. The state uses it to ensure that your business complies with local regulations and meets all necessary requirements to operate legally. Without it, your LLC simply cannot exist as a recognized entity. Think of it as your business's birth certificate—a formal acknowledgment from the state that your business is now alive and ready to engage in commerce.

As you prepare to draft this crucial document, it's important to understand the necessary elements that must be included. The Articles of Organization typically require you to provide the LLC's name, which must match the name you previously reserved, along with its physical address. This address is where official correspondence will be sent, so it needs to be accurate and up-to-date. Additionally, you must specify your LLC's management structure. This involves indicating whether your LLC will be member-managed or manager-managed. In a member-managed LLC, the owners are directly responsible for the operations, while a manager-managed LLC delegates operational responsibilities to appointed managers. This choice affects how your LLC operates daily and should align with your business strategy and needs. Other components might include the purpose of your business and the duration of its existence, although this can vary depending on your state's specific requirements.

Once you have meticulously prepared all the necessary information, it's time to submit your Articles of Organization to the appropriate state authority. The filing process can generally be completed either online or by mail. Online submissions are often quicker and more efficient, allowing you to complete the process through a state-specific filing portal. This method typically involves filling out a digital form and attaching any relevant supporting documents. On the other hand, if you prefer traditional methods, you can opt for mail-in submissions, which require you to print the completed forms and send them to the designated state office. Keep in mind that processing times can vary; online filings are usually processed faster, while mail-in submissions might take a bit longer.

Filing your Articles of Organization does come with associated costs, which are an important consideration as you plan your budget. State filing fees vary widely, typically ranging from $50 to several hundred dollars, depending on the state. It's crucial to research your specific state's fees to avoid any surprises. Additionally, if you're in a hurry to get your LLC up and running, many states offer expedited processing for an additional fee. This service can significantly reduce the waiting time, allowing your LLC to begin operations sooner rather than later. However, these expedited fees can add up, so weigh the urgency against your budget to make an informed choice. The costs associated with filing your Articles are an investment in your business's legal foundation, ensuring that you are compliant and ready to operate within the legal framework of your state.

Navigating the intricacies of drafting and filing your Articles of Organization is a fundamental step in the LLC formation process. It requires careful attention to detail, ensuring that all information is accurate and complete to avoid any potential setbacks or rejections from the state. By understanding the purpose and components of this document and by following the proper filing procedures, you lay a strong legal foundation for your LLC. This foundation is essential for establishing your business's legitimacy and ensuring that you can operate smoothly and legally in the marketplace.

Whilst it is possible to lodge and create these documents yourself, I suggest getting a lawyer or an LLC services business to help. They do this day in and day out and can suggest cheaper formation states, which reduce the costs of compliance. For example, you may know how to fix your own car, but a mechanic does it every day and will likely do a better job. Spend the money and get an expert to do it for you.

2.3 Navigating State-Specific Filing Requirements

Filing an LLC is not a one-size-fits-all process; it varies significantly from state to state. Each state has its own set of requirements, unique documentation needs, and specific forms that must be completed. For instance, while one state might require you to include detailed information about your LLC's management structure in the Articles of Organization, another might focus on different aspects such as the purpose of the business or member contributions. Understanding these variations is crucial because failing to comply with your state's specific requirements can lead to delays in the formation process or even rejection of your filings. It's like trying to fit a square peg into a round hole; you need the right tools for the job.

To effectively navigate these differences, it's important to leverage resources that provide state-specific guidance. First, look to your state's government websites, typically managed by the Secretary of State's office. These sites often offer comprehensive resources, including step-by-step guides for filing, downloadable forms, and FAQs that can answer many of your questions. Additionally, consulting legal advisory services can offer personalized insights into the nuanced requirements of your state. These professionals can help clarify any ambiguous requirements and ensure that your documentation is in order, so you can confidently move forward with your LLC formation.

Adhering to state-specific regulations is not just a bureaucratic formality; it's necessary to avoid legal complications that could arise from non-compliance. Failing to adhere to these regulations can result in fines, penalties, or, in severe cases, the inability to legally operate your business. Compliance ensures that your LLC is recognized as a legitimate entity and is protected under the law. Think of it as laying the groundwork for your business's legal and operational security. By understanding and following these regulations, you protect your business and set it up for future success.

Despite the best intentions, common mistakes during the filing process can happen. One frequent error is misunderstanding the form requirements. It's easy to overlook a section or misinterpret a question, leading to incomplete or incorrect submissions. This can be avoided by thoroughly reading and understanding each requirement before filling out the forms. Another common mistake is incorrect fee payments. States often have specific fee structures, and paying the wrong amount can delay processing or result in rejection. Double-checking fee requirements and ensuring accurate payment is a simple yet crucial step in the filing process. Such mistakes are not just minor inconveniences; they can cause significant delays in getting your LLC off the ground. By being meticulous and informed, you can avoid these pitfalls and ensure a smooth filing process.

Resource List: State-Specific Filing Resources

- **State Government Websites**: Visit your state's Secretary of State website for official filing forms and guidelines.
- **Legal Advisory Services**: Consider consulting a lawyer specializing in business formation to navigate complex state-specific requirements.
- **State Filing Portals**: Utilize online portals for a streamlined filing experience, often faster than traditional mail submissions.

Taking the time to understand and comply with state-specific filing requirements is a critical step in forming an LLC. It demands attention to detail and a willingness to seek out and utilize available resources. By doing so, you ensure that your business is prepared to operate legally and efficiently from day one.

2.4 Appointing a Registered Agent - Roles and Responsibilities

The role of a registered agent is a crucial aspect of your LLC's operational framework. At its core, a registered agent serves as the official point of contact for your LLC, tasked with the responsibility of receiving legal documents on behalf of the business. This includes service of process notices, government correspondence, and compliance-related documents. The registered agent ensures that you are always informed of any legal actions or requirements, acting as a reliable intermediary between your business and the state. This role is not just about receiving mail; it is about maintaining the line of communication that keeps your business in good legal standing.

For someone to qualify as a registered agent, they must meet specific criteria. Primarily, the registered agent must be a resident of the state where your LLC is registered or a business entity authorized to conduct business in that state.

This residency requirement ensures that the agent is physically present during normal business hours to receive any important documents. It's important to choose someone who is dependable and organized, as the timely management of legal documents is essential for your LLC's compliance and reputation. The agent's role is fundamental, not just for legal correspondence, but also for ensuring that compliance notices are handled promptly, safeguarding your business from potential legal complications.

When considering options for appointing a registered agent, you have a couple of viable paths. One option is to hire a professional registered agent service. These services offer the expertise and reliability that can be invaluable, particularly for those new to business ownership. Professional services ensure that you never miss a critical document, providing peace of mind and allowing you to focus on other aspects of running your business. Additionally, they offer privacy, as their address is listed in public records instead of yours. Alternatively, you may choose to appoint an internal member of your LLC, such as yourself or a trusted business partner. This approach can be cost-effective, but it requires a commitment to being available during business hours and managing the responsibility with diligence. Whichever option you choose, it's essential to weigh the pros and cons and consider what best aligns with your business needs and resources.

Changing your registered agent is a straightforward process, but requires adherence to specific protocols to ensure compliance. If you decide to switch agents, whether due to dissatisfaction with current services or a change in business operations, you must file the appropriate change of agent forms with your state. Each state has its own procedure for this, typically involving a formal notification and possibly a fee. The new agent must meet the state's qualifications, and the change must be officially recorded to update your LLC's public records. This process ensures that your business remains compliant and that all legal documents continue to reach you without interruption.

Understanding the role and responsibilities of a registered agent is fundamental in maintaining your LLC's operational integrity. By carefully selecting an agent and adhering to state requirements, you protect your business from legal pitfalls and ensure smooth communication with state authorities. The registered agent is, in many ways, the unsung hero of your LLC, quietly ensuring that your business runs smoothly and remains compliant.

2.5 Creating an Operating Agreement – Your Business Blueprint

Creating an Operating Agreement for your LLC is akin to drafting the blueprint of your business. It is a document that outlines the structure, responsibilities, and operational procedures of your LLC, acting as a guide for all members involved. Even if your state doesn't require one, having an Operating Agreement is invaluable. It clarifies management roles and sets expectations, serving as a preemptive measure against misunderstandings and disputes. When everyone knows their role and how decisions are made, the potential for conflict diminishes significantly. For instance, in a multi-member LLC, one member might be responsible for financial oversight, while another focuses on marketing strategies. By delineating these roles clearly, you create a harmonious operational environment where each member knows their specific contributions and obligations.

The key components of an Operating Agreement are the backbone of its effectiveness. Ownership percentages are critical, as they determine the extent of each member's stake in the company, influencing voting rights and profit distribution. These percentages should reflect each member's contribution to the business, whether in capital, expertise, or time. Voting rights and procedures are another essential aspect of the agreement. Establishing clear guidelines on how decisions are made and the weight each vote carries ensures that the decision-making process is transparent and democratic. For example, while some decisions might require a simple majority, others might necessitate a unanimous vote. Additionally, profit distribution must be outlined, detailing how and when profits will be shared among members. Will profits be reinvested into the business or distributed at regular intervals? Addressing these questions within the Operating Agreement prevents future disagreements and promotes financial clarity.

To assist you in drafting an Operating Agreement, utilizing templates and examples can be immensely helpful. These resources provide a foundation upon which you can build a customized agreement that suits your LLC's unique needs. Sample clauses for voting and decision-making can offer insights into how other businesses structure their agreements, providing a benchmark for your own. However, remember that templates are starting points; your final document should reflect the specific dynamics and goals of your LLC. Consulting with a legal professional to review your agreement can further ensure that it is comprehensive and legally sound.

Operating without a formal agreement opens the door to a host of risks and challenges. Without clear guidelines, the potential for member disputes increases significantly. Imagine a scenario where two members disagree on the direction of a project. Without an agreement, there is no established process for resolving such disputes, leading to potential stalemates or even legal battles. Furthermore, the absence of an Operating Agreement means a lack of clear operational guidelines. This ambiguity can result in inefficiencies and a lack of accountability, as members may have differing interpretations of their roles and responsibilities. The Operating Agreement acts as a safeguard against such pitfalls, providing a structured framework that promotes unity and efficiency.

As you conclude this chapter, reflect on the comprehensive nature of forming an LLC. From choosing a business name to appointing a registered agent, each step is crucial in establishing a solid foundation for your business. Creating an Operating Agreement is no different; it solidifies your LLC's internal structure and prepares you for success. With this blueprint in place, you are ready to move forward with confidence, knowing that your LLC is built on a bedrock of clarity and cooperation.

Don't move on to the next chapter without doing the following;

1. Do you have any questions that need answering about LLC formation? Write them down to ask the expert you get to help you set it up
2. Need a business loan to help with startup cash flow? Check out NerdWallet

for the best options

3. Chosen a name? Check it out in the state you're forming it in, their Secretary of State's website, the US Patent and Trademark Office website, and then Google it to see what comes up. Don't go up against someone with the same name, it just means legal battles and having to change your name down the track. At this stage, I also check on website domain sites, like GoDaddy, to see if the website is available, preferably with a .com website domain

4. Jot down some points you want included in your Operating Agreement, including roles and responsibilities, profit structure, voting decisions, and any other important information so whoever is drafting it for you can use this as a starting point.

Chapter 3

Financial and Tax Strategies for LLCs

Imagine you're sitting at your desk, coffee in hand, staring at a mountain of financial paperwork. You've taken the plunge into entrepreneurship, but now you're faced with a new challenge: taxes. Navigating the world of LLC taxation can feel like deciphering a foreign language. However, understanding these financial intricacies is crucial to your business's success. As a CPA, I've seen firsthand how pass-through taxation can be a game-changer for small business owners. It's a concept that might seem daunting at first, but once you grasp its nuances, it becomes an invaluable tool in your financial arsenal.

Pass-through taxation is one of the most significant advantages of forming an LLC, especially for those who are wary of the complexities associated with corporate taxes. At its core, pass-through taxation means that your LLC itself does not pay income taxes as an entity. Instead, the income "passes through" to you and any other owners, who then report it on personal tax returns. This approach avoids the dreaded double taxation that corporations face, where income is taxed at both the corporate and personal levels. By only taxing income once, at the individual level, you potentially save a substantial amount of money, enabling you to reinvest more back into your business or set aside for future growth.

The distribution of income and losses among LLC members is another crucial aspect of this taxation model. Typically, income is distributed prorata, meaning it's divided according to each member's ownership percentage. For instance, if you own 60% of the LLC, you would receive 60% of the income or bear 60% of the losses. However, your Operating Agreement can allow for special allocations if it aligns with the business's needs and all members agree. This flexibility can be particularly beneficial for businesses with varying contributions from each member, allowing for a distribution model that reflects the actual dynamics of your partnership and rewards those contributing more to the LLC's success.

While pass-through taxation simplifies many aspects of tax reporting, it also introduces some unique considerations, particularly regarding self-employment taxes. As an LLC member, you are generally considered self-employed, which means you're responsible for paying self-employment taxes on your share of the LLC's income. This tax covers Social Security and Medicare contributions, and it's calculated at a rate of 15.3% of your net earnings. The good news is that you can deduct half of this self-employment tax when calculating your adjusted gross income, softening the financial impact. This deduction effectively reduces your taxable income, providing some relief as you manage the dual roles of employee and employer.

The IRS's classification of LLCs for tax purposes adds another layer to this financial landscape. By default, a single-member LLC is considered a disregarded entity, meaning its income and expenses are reported on the owner's personal tax return, similar to a sole proprietorship. Multi-member LLCs are treated as partnerships, requiring the filing of a partnership tax return. However, LLCs have the flexibility to elect to be taxed as a corporation if advantageous. This is done by filing Form 8832, and if electing S-Corp status, also Form 2553. Each classification has its benefits and drawbacks, depending on your financial situation and business goals.

OK, that last paragraph was a lot. Don't freak out just yet! This is a high-level overview. We'll go through the specifics throughout this chapter. OK, let's keep going.

Reflection Section: Navigating Tax Decisions

Consider your own business structure and financial goals. Reflect on how pass-through taxation impacts your tax strategy. Are you taking full advantage of the deductions available to you? How does your current IRS classification align with your business objectives? Write down any insights or questions that arise, and use them to inform your next steps in optimizing your LLC's financial strategy.

Understanding and leveraging pass-through taxation is a critical step in ensuring your LLC's financial health, allowing you to focus on growing your business with confidence and clarity.

3.1 Essential Bookkeeping Practices for LLC Owners

Imagine you're sitting at your desk, surrounded by receipts and invoices, wondering how to make sense of it all. Bookkeeping might not be the most glamorous part of running a business, but it's undeniably one of the most important. For LLC owners, embracing strong bookkeeping practices is crucial to maintaining financial health and compliance. The double-entry accounting system forms the backbone of these practices. This system ensures that every financial transaction is recorded in at least two accounts, providing a comprehensive view of your business's financial position. It helps track where your money is coming from and where it's going. This clarity is invaluable, especially during tax season or when seeking funding. Accurate record-keeping is your ally here, enabling you to manage your finances effectively and avoid costly mistakes.

In today's digital age, there's no need to rely solely on paper trails and manual calculations. Bookkeeping software can be a game-changer for LLC owners, streamlining financial tracking and reporting. QuickBooks, often hailed as the go-to solution for small businesses, offers a suite of features that simplify everything from invoicing to payroll. Its intuitive interface allows you to manage your finances without needing an accounting degree. For freelancers and sole traders, FreshBooks is another excellent option. It's specifically designed to cater to the needs of smaller operations, offering tools like time tracking and expense management. These software solutions not only save time but also reduce the likelihood of human error, ensuring your financial records are always accurate and up to date.

Maintaining essential financial records is a non-negotiable aspect of effective bookkeeping. Receipts and invoices are the bread and butter of your financial documentation. They provide evidence of your business transactions, supporting your income and expense claims. Keeping organized records of these documents is vital, as they form the basis of your financial statements and tax filings. Bank statements are equally important, offering a snapshot of your cash flow and helping you track your financial habits. They serve as a powerful tool for identifying trends, such as periods of high or low income, allowing you to plan accordingly. And, of course, tax documents are critical, encompassing everything from past returns to forms related to deductions and credits. Having these records readily accessible can make tax season less stressful and more efficient.

However, even with the best intentions, bookkeeping errors can occur, and they can have serious repercussions. One common mistake is mixing personal and business expenses. It's an easy trap to fall into, especially for sole proprietors or freelancers working from home. However, failing to separate these expenses can lead to inaccurate financial reporting and complicate tax filings. Maintaining a dedicated business account helps mitigate this risk, ensuring a clear separation between personal and business finances. Another frequent error is failing to reconcile accounts monthly. Reconciling involves comparing your financial records with your bank statements to ensure they match. Neglecting this step can result in discrepancies going unnoticed, potentially leading to unintentional tax errors or financial mismanagement.

Call to Action: Reinforce Your Bookkeeping

Take a moment to assess your current bookkeeping practices. Are you using software to streamline your processes? Do you have a system in place for organizing receipts and invoices? Consider investing in accounting software if you haven't already, and set a monthly reminder to reconcile your accounts. By proactively managing your bookkeeping, you set a strong foundation for your LLC's financial success.

While bookkeeping may not be the most exciting task, it is undoubtedly a critical one. By implementing robust practices and utilizing modern tools, you can ensure your LLC's financial records are accurate and insightful, paving the way for informed business decisions. If you are 100% terrible with numbers, then I suggest, in the early stages, hiring a bookkeeper so they can look after the numbers for you and create the filings you'll need. You do need to be good with numbers as you grow as a manager, so use it as a stepping stone to learn as you go. Ask questions so that you can broaden your knowledge base - there are no dumb questions!

3.2 Tax Deductions and Credits – Maximizing Your Benefits

Understanding tax deductions is like finding hidden treasure in the world of business expenses. For an LLC, these deductions can significantly reduce your taxable income, leaving more money in your pocket to reinvest in your business or to reward your hard work with a little more breathing room. One of the most common deductions is for home office expenses, which can be a game-changer for freelancers and sole traders who operate primarily from their homes. If a portion of your home is dedicated exclusively to business activities, you can deduct a percentage of your rent or mortgage, utilities, and even home insurance. This deduction reflects the cost of running a business from the comfort of your home, making the line between personal and business expenses a little clearer.

Travel and entertainment costs are another area ripe for deductions. If your business requires travel—whether it's meeting clients in different cities or attending industry conferences—those associated expenses can be deducted. This includes transportation, lodging, and meals. However, it's essential to remember that only 50% of meal expenses are typically deductible, so keeping detailed records is crucial. Similarly, entertainment costs related directly to business activities can also be deducted, though recent tax law changes have tightened the criteria for these expenses. Keep in mind, the key is that these costs must be ordinary and necessary for your business.

Health insurance premiums can also be deducted if you're self-employed. This is particularly beneficial for those who don't have coverage through a spouse's employer. The premiums for medical, dental, and long-term care insurance can be deducted, offering substantial savings. However, this deduction is only available if you are not eligible for a subsidized health plan and have a net profit for the year. It's a deduction that not only helps financially but also encourages maintaining health coverage, which is vital for any business owner aiming for longevity and success.

While deductions reduce your taxable income, tax credits directly reduce the amount of tax you owe, making them exceptionally valuable. The research and development credit is one such incentive, encouraging businesses to innovate and improve their products or processes. If your LLC is engaged in activities that seek to develop a new or improved business component, this credit could apply. Similarly, the energy efficiency credit rewards businesses that invest in energy-saving improvements. Whether upgrading to energy-efficient appliances or implementing sustainable practices, these credits not only reduce your tax liability but also contribute positively to the environment.

To successfully claim these deductions and credits, meticulous documentation is paramount. Keep every receipt, invoice, and bank statement that substantiates your claims. Detailed records not only support your deductions but also protect you in the event of an audit. A well-organized system for maintaining these documents will save you countless headaches during tax time, allowing you to focus on what you do best—running your business. This approach ensures that every dollar you're entitled to save is accounted for, enhancing your cash flow and financial stability.

Another tax strategy available to LLCs is the use of loss carry forwards. If your business incurs a net operating loss (NOL), you can carry this loss forward to offset future taxable income. This means that if you experience a tough financial year, you can use that loss to reduce your tax burden when business picks up again. The rules for carrying forward losses can be complex, often requiring a tax professional's guidance to navigate, but the potential tax savings make it well worth exploring. Understanding how these tools work and integrating them into your tax planning can provide your LLC with a crucial financial buffer, helping to stabilize cash flow and support sustainable growth.

3.3 Common Tax Mistakes and How to Avoid Them

Navigating the tax landscape is a critical responsibility for any LLC owner. Yet, it's an area where errors frequently occur, often leading to costly repercussions. One common misstep is misreporting income, which can happen when financial records aren't meticulously maintained or when there's a misunderstanding of what constitutes taxable income. This mistake can trigger audits, penalties, and interest charges, placing an undue financial burden on your business. To avoid this pitfall, ensure that every income source is accurately tracked and reported. Implementing a reliable financial tracking system, whether through dedicated software or manual records, is pivotal. Regularly cross-checking these records against bank statements can further help in maintaining accuracy.

Another prevalent issue is missing tax deadlines. With the myriad of responsibilities that come with running an LLC, it's easy to overlook filing dates. However, late filings can lead to penalties and interest, affecting your cash flow. The solution lies in proactive calendar management. Mark key dates well in advance, and set reminders a few weeks before deadlines to ensure you're prepared. Some business owners find it helpful to delegate this task to a dedicated team member or to use automated tools that send alerts as deadlines approach. By staying ahead of the timeline, you can avoid the stress and financial impact of missed deadlines.

The classification of workers is another area riddled with potential errors. Misclassifying employees as independent contractors is a mistake that can lead to severe penalties from the IRS. This misclassification often arises from a lack of understanding of the distinctions between an employee, who is on payroll and eligible for benefits, and an independent contractor, who operates as a separate entity. The IRS scrutinizes these classifications closely, and errors can result in back taxes, fines, and legal fees. To prevent this, familiarize yourself with the specific criteria for each classification. Consider consulting with a tax professional to ensure your workforce is correctly categorized, thereby safeguarding your business from unnecessary legal and financial complications.

Underpayment of estimated taxes is another challenge that can catch LLC owners off guard. Since LLCs are often pass-through entities, owners must pay estimated taxes on their share of the business income. Failing to pay enough can lead to penalties when tax time rolls around. To mitigate this risk, calculate your estimated taxes based on last year's income, or better yet, adjust them quarterly based on current earnings. The IRS's safe harbor rules can provide guidance, allowing you to avoid penalties if you pay at least 90% of the current year's taxes or 100% of the previous year's liability. Regularly reviewing your tax situation with an accountant can provide the clarity needed to avoid underpayments.

Poor record-keeping is a silent yet pervasive issue that can escalate into significant problems if left unchecked. Inadequate documentation not only complicates tax filing but also increases the risk of audits. An audit can be time-consuming and stressful, potentially uncovering errors that could have been easily avoided with proper records. Maintain a robust system for organizing all financial documents, from receipts to invoices, and ensure they are readily accessible. Regular audits of your records, either internally or with a professional's assistance, can preemptively identify and correct discrepancies. This proactive approach builds a solid defense against audits and ensures your business's financial integrity remains intact.

3.4 State-Specific Tax Regulations – What You Need to Know

Tax obligations for LLCs can vary significantly from one state to another, adding a layer of complexity to managing your business's finances. Understanding these differences is crucial for ensuring compliance and optimizing your tax strategy. At the state level, income taxes are often imposed, and they can differ in terms of rates and application. Some states, like Texas and Wyoming, don't levy a personal income tax, which might influence where you choose to establish your LLC. However, these states might have other taxes or higher fees elsewhere to compensate. On the other hand, states like California have higher income taxes, which can impact your bottom line and require careful planning to avoid surprises at tax time.

Franchise taxes or fees are another consideration, as they can apply regardless of whether your LLC turns a profit. These are not related to business franchises as one might expect but are instead fees for the privilege of doing business in a state. The structure and amount of these taxes vary widely. For example, California charges an $800 minimum franchise tax, while Delaware calculates its franchise tax based on the company's authorized shares or assumed par value capital. Understanding these obligations is critical, as failing to pay them can lead to penalties or even the suspension of your LLC's ability to operate.

To stay compliant with state-specific tax requirements, it's essential to register your LLC with the state's tax authorities upon formation. This step ensures that you receive all necessary tax notifications and are recognized as a legitimate business entity within the state. Regular state tax filings are also a key part of maintaining compliance. These filings may include income tax returns, franchise tax reports, and sales tax filings, depending on your business activities and the state's requirements. Keeping up with these filings is crucial, as missed deadlines can result in penalties that add up quickly, eating into your profits.

For businesses operating in multiple states, understanding the concept of "nexus" is vital. Nexus refers to the connection or presence a business has in a state, which can trigger tax obligations beyond the state of incorporation. If your LLC sells goods or services in multiple states, you may need to collect sales tax in those states if you have a physical presence, employees, or significant sales there. The rules for establishing nexus vary, so it's important to review each state's specific regulations to determine your responsibilities. Additionally, apportionment of income might be necessary when your business activities span several states. This process involves dividing your income among the states where you operate, based on factors such as sales, property, and payroll.

Navigating state-specific tax regulations can be daunting, but there are resources available to help you manage this complexity. State Department of Revenue websites are a valuable starting point, often providing detailed information on tax rates, forms, and filing deadlines specific to each state. These websites are usually updated regularly, ensuring you have access to the latest information. Additionally, consulting with professional tax advisors who specialize in state tax compliance can offer personalized guidance tailored to your business's circumstances. These advisors can help interpret complex regulations, identify potential tax savings, and ensure that your LLC remains in good standing with all applicable state requirements. By leveraging these resources, you can confidently navigate the complexities of state taxation and focus on growing your business.

3.5 Financial Planning for Long-Term Success

Planning for long-term success in your LLC is about more than just managing day-to-day finances; it requires a strategic approach to budgeting and growth. One effective budgeting strategy is zero-based budgeting, which starts from scratch each period, requiring you to justify every expense. This method can help eliminate unnecessary costs and ensure that every dollar spent contributes directly to your business goals. By examining each expense closely, you gain insight into your financial health, allowing for better allocation of resources. This approach is particularly beneficial in rapidly changing industries where adaptability is key. Additionally, rolling forecasts offer another layer of financial foresight. By continuously updating your forecast based on actual performance, you can adjust quickly to market changes and unexpected challenges, ensuring your budget aligns with real-world conditions. This is the preferred approach for a more established business.

Cash flow is the lifeblood of any business, and managing it effectively is crucial for sustainability. Creating cash flow forecasts allows you to predict and plan for future cash needs, helping you avoid shortfalls and seize opportunities as they arise. Regularly updating these forecasts with real-time data provides a dynamic view of your financial landscape, enabling proactive decision-making. Moreover, maintaining a cash reserve acts as a financial safety net, buffering against unforeseen expenses or dips in revenue. This reserve can be a lifeline during lean periods or economic downturns, providing the stability needed to weather financial storms. For many business owners, the peace of mind that comes from having a cash cushion cannot be overstated, allowing you to focus on strategic growth rather than survival.

Investing in your LLC's growth is a critical component of long-term success. Reinvesting profits back into the business can drive expansion and innovation. Capital expenditures on new equipment or technology can enhance productivity and open new revenue streams. Similarly, hiring additional staff can increase capacity and allow you to take on more clients or projects. However, investment should be strategic, aligned with your long-term vision and market opportunities. Assessing the potential return on investment for each expenditure helps ensure that resources are used wisely, supporting sustainable growth rather than stretching your finances thin. Ensure these are included in your cash flow forecast so you're not stretched too thin.

Retirement planning is a critical yet often overlooked aspect of long-term financial health for business owners. As a self-employed individual, traditional employer-sponsored retirement plans may not be available, but options like SEP IRAs and Solo 401(k) plans offer robust alternatives. These plans provide tax advantages and the flexibility to contribute significant amounts annually, helping secure your financial future. Planning for retirement early allows you to take advantage of compound growth, ensuring that you can transition out of your business when the time is right, without financial strain. It's about creating a future where you can enjoy the fruits of your labor, knowing your financial security is assured. It is also a tax deduction when the cash flow timing works for the business.

Risk management strategies are essential for protecting your business from unforeseen challenges. Business insurance is a fundamental component, safeguarding against liabilities and potential losses. From general liability to professional indemnity, having the right coverage is crucial.

Additionally, diversifying revenue streams can provide stability, reducing reliance on a single source of income. This diversification allows your business to remain resilient, even if one area faces a downturn. By spreading risk across various channels, you create a robust financial structure capable of withstanding market fluctuations and unexpected disruptions. Consult an insurance broker who can advise on the best insurance needed. You should insure what you can't afford to lose, so think about that once you get your insurance quotes through.

In planning for the future, each of these strategies plays a pivotal role in ensuring your business not only survives but thrives. By implementing effective budgeting, managing cash flow, investing wisely, planning for retirement, and mitigating risks, you lay the groundwork for a prosperous future. This comprehensive approach to financial planning is not just about immediate gains but about securing long-term success in an ever-evolving business landscape. As you move forward, these principles will guide your decisions, helping you build a resilient and thriving LLC.

Don't move on to the next chapter without doing the following;

1. Have you chosen accounting software? If you don't have one currently, then choose between QuickBooks, FreshBooks, or Xero. They're all good beginner-level software packages
2. Do you have a tax filing calendar? Put it in your diary and then also diarize

a week before the due date to review if things have started/progressed

3. Contact an insurance broker to understand what insurance you may need and when. Search http:/www.trustedchoice.com/agents to find a broker in your state and postcode

4. Do you have a list of questions you've been writing down to ask your accountant? Keep adding to this list as I'm sure you'll have more questions as we keep going

Chapter 4

Legal Compliance and Maintenance

When I first glanced at the vast landscape of business compliance, it felt like trying to decode an ancient script. Legal compliance seemed like a daunting maze, full of potential pitfalls and hidden costs. Yet, as I delved deeper, I realized that understanding and maintaining compliance is not just about ticking boxes. It's about safeguarding your business, ensuring its longevity, and building trust with your clients and partners. For many of you—business people, sole traders, freelancers, and publishers—the notion of compliance might appear abstract, but it's fundamentally about protecting what you've worked hard to build. It's about ensuring that your LLC not only thrives but also operates within the framework that the law requires, paving the way for sustainable success.

4.1 Annual Reporting Requirements – Staying Compliant

Annual reports are a key element in maintaining the good standing of your LLC. They serve as a public declaration of your company's ongoing activities, affirming your commitment to transparency and accountability. These reports provide the state with critical information about your business, ensuring that your company remains compliant with state laws and regulations. By filing an annual report, you communicate that your LLC is active, engaged, and operational, thereby preserving its legal status and credibility. Public disclosure of company information is not merely a formality; it's a demonstration of your business's integrity and commitment to trustworthiness.

Typically, an annual report must include updated details about your LLC, reflecting any changes or developments over the past year. This begins with your business address, which must be current and accurate to ensure seamless communication with state authorities. If your address has changed, it's crucial to update this information in your annual report to avoid missed correspondence. Similarly, the names and addresses of your LLC's members or managers must be included, providing a clear picture of who is responsible for the company's management and operations. This transparency is essential for stakeholders, including investors, partners, and customers, who rely on accurate information to make informed decisions about their engagement with your business. Additionally, the details of your registered agent, who serves as your official point of contact for legal matters, must be included. Ensuring this information is up-to-date is vital for maintaining compliance and ensuring that legal documents reach you without delay.

Filing your annual report can be done through various methods, and it's important to choose the one that aligns best with your preferences and capacities. Many states offer the convenience of online submissions via state websites, providing a streamlined process that saves time and reduces the likelihood of errors. This method often allows for faster processing and immediate confirmation of receipt, which can be comforting in knowing your compliance obligations are met. Alternatively, traditional mail-in options are available for those who prefer a more tactile approach. These require you to print the necessary forms, fill them out manually, and submit them via post. While this method may take longer, it can be ideal for those who appreciate having physical copies for their records.

Meeting deadlines for annual report submissions is crucial, as failure to do so can lead to significant consequences for your LLC. Each state sets specific deadlines for filing these reports, and missing them can result in penalties, fines, or even administrative dissolution. The latter is a severe penalty, where the state revokes your LLC's legal status, rendering it unable to operate legally. To prevent this, it's essential to be aware of your state's specific filing requirements and deadlines. Some states, like California, require annual reports to be filed by the last day of the anniversary month of your LLC's incorporation, while others, like Arkansas, have specific deadlines for franchise tax reports. Familiarize yourself with these dates and mark them on your calendar to ensure timely compliance.

Reflection Section: Ensuring Compliance

Take a moment to reflect on your current compliance practices. Consider whether you have a reliable system in place to track your LLC's annual report deadlines and whether your business information is up-to-date. Are there areas where your compliance strategy can be improved? Consider setting a reminder to review your compliance status regularly, ensuring that your LLC remains in good standing with the state.

4.2 Maintaining an LLC's Legal Protections

Running your LLC is not just about the day-to-day operations; it's also about safeguarding the very structure that allows your business to thrive. One of the cardinal rules in maintaining your LLC's legal protections is ensuring a clear separation between personal and business activities. This separation begins with having distinct business bank accounts. Never underestimate the significance of this step. By keeping your business finances separate, you avoid commingling funds—a risky practice that could jeopardize your limited liability protection. Imagine trying to untangle a ball of yarn, each thread representing a different financial transaction. Without separation, your personal and business finances become indistinguishably intertwined, increasing the risk of personal liability in the event of legal action against your

LLC. It's not just a matter of convenience; it's a legal safeguard.

Thorough documentation and record-keeping are vital to fortifying your LLC's legal standing. Keeping detailed meeting minutes for any member decisions is not just a formality; it's your LLC's history in written form. These records can provide clarity and evidence of intent, should disputes arise among members or with external parties. Similarly, having well-drafted contracts and agreements is paramount. These documents outline the terms of business relationships and can prevent misunderstandings that might lead to costly legal battles. They serve as the backbone of your business operations, ensuring that everyone involved understands their roles and obligations. This proactive approach to documentation not only protects your LLC but also builds trust with partners and clients, reinforcing your reputation as a responsible and reliable business entity.

As your business evolves, your legal documents must evolve with it. Regular updates to key documents are necessary to reflect changes in your business's circumstances. For instance, your Operating Agreement—the road map of your LLC's operations—should be amended to include any significant changes in management structure or operational procedures. Failing to update this document can lead to confusion and potential conflicts, undermining the very foundation of your business. Similarly, updating your Articles of Organization with the state ensures that your LLC's public records accurately reflect its current status. This transparency is crucial for maintaining good standing with regulatory authorities and for informing stakeholders of your business's ongoing activities.

Handling changes in membership or management requires careful attention to detail and adherence to established procedures. When a member decides to leave the LLC or when new members join, it's essential to have a buy-sell agreement in place. This agreement outlines the terms under which members can buy or sell their stakes in the company, providing a clear path for ownership transitions. Without it, disputes over valuation and rights can arise, potentially leading to internal friction and operational disruption. Equally important are formal resignation procedures for departing members. These procedures ensure a smooth transition and continuity of operations, allowing the LLC to adapt seamlessly to changes in its management team. By establishing clear protocols for membership changes, you not only protect the interests of your LLC but also foster a stable and supportive environment for all members involved.

Navigating the complexities of maintaining an LLC's legal protections can seem overwhelming, but each step you take reinforces the strength and resilience of your business. By maintaining a clear separation of finances, committing to meticulous documentation, updating legal documents as necessary, and establishing procedures for membership changes, you create a robust framework that supports your LLC's growth and stability. This proactive approach to legal maintenance not only safeguards your business today but also lays the groundwork for future success, ensuring that your LLC remains a strong and credible entity in the eyes of partners, clients, and regulatory bodies alike.

4.3 Understanding and Managing Compliance Deadlines

In the life of an LLC, compliance deadlines are the markers that keep your business aligned with legal obligations. They are not merely dates on a calendar but pivotal points that ensure your LLC remains in good standing. One of the most critical deadlines is the annual report filing. Each year, your LLC must submit this document, which serves as a confirmation of your ongoing business activities and updates any changes in your business structure. It's a yearly check-in with the state, affirming that your business is still operational and compliant. Equally important are tax payment dates. These are the deadlines by which your business must pay any owed taxes, including state and federal income taxes, sales taxes, and any applicable franchise taxes. Missing these dates can have dire consequences, so it's vital to have them prominently marked and managed.

Creating a compliance calendar is an effective strategy for staying on top of these critical deadlines. In today's digital age, there's no shortage of tools available to help you organize and track important dates. Digital calendar tools like Google Calendar or Microsoft Outlook can serve as central hubs for all your compliance-related activities. They allow you to set reminders, color-code different types of deadlines, and even share the calendar with your team to ensure everyone is on the same page. Incorporating reminder systems is also beneficial. These can be simple alerts set weeks or days before the deadline, giving you ample time to prepare and act. By integrating these tools into your routine, staying compliant becomes a seamless part of your business operations, reducing the risk of oversights and last-minute scrambles.

The repercussions of missed deadlines extend beyond mere inconvenience. Failing to meet compliance obligations can lead to severe penalties, including administrative dissolution. This is a drastic measure where the state revokes your LLC's legal status, effectively shutting down your business. The process of reinstatement is not only cumbersome but also costly, often involving hefty reinstatement fees and the risk of losing business during the downtime. Moreover, missed deadlines can tarnish your business reputation, impacting relationships with clients, vendors, and financial institutions. Consistently meeting compliance deadlines is a testament to your business's reliability and professionalism, fostering trust and confidence among stakeholders.

To ensure you stay organized and compliant, consider implementing a few practical strategies. Designating a compliance officer within your LLC can be a game-changer. This person is responsible for overseeing compliance activities, keeping track of upcoming deadlines, and ensuring that filings and payments are completed on time. They act as a watchdog, preventing any compliance-related issues from slipping through the cracks. Additionally, scheduling regular compliance reviews is a proactive measure to catch potential problems before they escalate. These reviews, whether monthly or quarterly, involve checking your compliance calendar, verifying that all obligations have been met, and assessing any upcoming requirements. This systematic approach not only keeps you on track but also provides peace of mind, knowing that your LLC is operating within the legal framework.

Call to Action: Implement Your Compliance Strategy

Take a moment to assess your current approach to managing compliance deadlines. Do you have a calendar set up with all necessary dates clearly marked? Have you designated a compliance officer, or are you tracking these obligations yourself? Consider implementing these strategies today to safeguard your LLC's legal standing and maintain its reputation as a responsible business.

4.4 Avoiding Common Legal Pitfalls in LLC Management

For many LLC owners, navigating the legal landscape is like walking a tightrope. It's a delicate balance of maintaining compliance while ensuring that the business operations run smoothly. One of the most frequent legal challenges that LLCs face is the failure to adhere to the Operating Agreement. This document is the backbone of your business, outlining the rights and responsibilities of each member. Yet, it's often neglected, leading to disputes that can disrupt your operations. Imagine a scenario where a decision is made that goes against the agreed terms. The lack of adherence can create confusion, upset members, and fracture trust. Clearly defined roles within the Operating Agreement can prevent such chaos. When everyone understands their duties, there's less room for conflict and more space for productive collaboration.

Another common pitfall is unclear member roles and responsibilities. When roles are not well-defined, it can lead to inefficiencies and friction. Members might step on each other's toes, resulting in duplicated efforts or missed tasks. This can be particularly disastrous in a small business where resources are limited. To avoid this, ensure that your Operating Agreement clearly delineates the roles of each member. Regular meetings can also help clarify responsibilities and keep everyone aligned with the business's goals. Think of it as setting the stage for a play—each actor knows their part, ensuring a seamless performance.

The importance of legal counsel cannot be overstated. In a world where laws and regulations are constantly evolving, having access to professional legal advice is invaluable. Retaining a business attorney can help you navigate complex issues and provide guidance on best practices for compliance. It's like having a guide who knows the terrain, helping you avoid potential pitfalls. Periodic legal audits can further ensure that your business remains compliant with all applicable laws. These audits can identify areas of risk and allow you to address them before they become significant problems. Consider it a health check for your business, ensuring that everything is running as it should.

Relying on informal agreements can be a recipe for disaster. While verbal agreements or handshake deals might seem convenient, they lack the enforceability of written contracts. Without documentation, misunderstandings can arise, leading to disputes that could have been easily avoided. Written contracts provide clarity, outlining the terms and conditions of any business arrangement. They serve as a reference point, ensuring that all parties understand their obligations. It's not just about protecting your interests; it's about fostering trust and professionalism in your business dealings. Having a solid contract in place can prevent issues before they escalate, saving you time and resources.

When conflicts do arise, having a strategy for resolution is key. Mediation and arbitration clauses can offer a structured process for resolving disputes without resorting to litigation. These methods are often less adversarial and more cost-effective than going to court. They provide a platform for both parties to express their concerns and work towards a mutually agreeable solution. Member voting procedures can also play a role in conflict resolution. By having a clear process for decision-making, you can ensure that all voices are heard and that disputes are resolved democratically. This approach not only resolves conflicts but also strengthens the bonds between members, fostering a collaborative and supportive environment.

Navigating the complexities of LLC management requires vigilance, foresight, and a commitment to best practices. By addressing common legal challenges head-on, you can ensure that your business remains compliant, efficient, and harmonious. It's about creating a solid foundation upon which your LLC can grow and thrive.

4.5 Adapting to Changes in State Laws and Regulations

Navigating the world of state regulations can feel like steering through shifting sands. Just when you think you've mastered the lay of the land, new laws can emerge, altering the landscape entirely. For an LLC, these regulatory changes are more than just bureaucratic updates—they can significantly impact your operations and strategy. Changes in tax legislation, for instance, can alter how your income is taxed or introduce new deductions and credits that could benefit your business. Similarly, revised filing procedures might streamline processes, reducing the time and effort required to maintain compliance. Staying attuned to these changes is not just beneficial; it's crucial for ensuring your business remains agile and competitive.

To keep your LLC in sync with the latest legal developments, proactive monitoring is key. Subscribing to legal bulletins is a practical way to receive timely updates about regulatory changes. These bulletins, often issued by legal firms or business associations, provide concise, relevant information that helps you stay informed without overwhelming you with legal jargon. Another effective strategy is joining industry associations. These organizations not only offer resources and networking opportunities but also keep their members updated on pertinent legal changes. Being part of such a community means having access to a wealth of knowledge and expertise, allowing you to anticipate changes and adjust your strategies accordingly.

Implementing changes in response to new regulations can seem daunting, but with the right approach, it becomes a manageable task. Start by updating your internal policies to reflect the new legal requirements. This might involve revising your compliance manuals or adapting your operational procedures to align with the latest standards. Training sessions for compliance are also invaluable. By educating your team about the changes and their implications, you ensure everyone is on the same page and can implement the necessary adjustments smoothly. These sessions can be conducted in-house or through external workshops, depending on the complexity of the changes and the expertise available within your LLC.

Appointing a dedicated compliance officer within your LLC can further streamline the adaptation process. This person acts as the central figure responsible for monitoring regulations, implementing changes, and ensuring ongoing compliance. The benefits of having a compliance officer are manifold. They provide a focused approach to managing legal adherence, allowing other members of your team to concentrate on their core responsibilities. Moreover, a compliance officer can act as a liaison with legal experts, ensuring your LLC receives accurate advice and guidance. This role is particularly valuable in industries that are heavily regulated or subject to frequent changes, where maintaining compliance is not only a legal obligation but also a competitive advantage.

As I reflect on the importance of staying current with legal changes, I recall a conversation with a fellow entrepreneur who faced significant challenges due to regulatory shifts. Her business had thrived under previous tax laws, but when new legislation was introduced, it dramatically altered her financial landscape. It was a tough lesson, but it underscored the importance of vigilance and adaptability. By embracing changes and integrating them into your operations, you not only safeguard your LLC but also position it for long-term success. The legal environment will continue to evolve, but with the right strategies and resources, your LLC can navigate these changes with confidence and resilience.

4.6 Utilizing Legal Tools and Resources for LLCs

Navigating the legal landscape of running an LLC can often feel like a complex puzzle. However, with the right tools and resources, maintaining compliance and ensuring your business's legal health becomes significantly more manageable. Online compliance platforms are among the most valuable tools available today. These platforms streamline the process of tracking compliance requirements, offering reminders for critical filing deadlines, and providing access to essential forms and documents. By using such platforms, you can automate many of the tedious aspects of legal compliance, freeing up time to focus on growing your business. Document management software complements these platforms by organizing and storing all your important legal documents in one secure location. This software makes it easy to retrieve documents when needed, ensuring that you never misplace a crucial contract or agreement. Together, these tools not only enhance efficiency but also bolster your LLC's legal standing by ensuring that all compliance obligations are met in a timely manner.

In addition to practical tools, continuing education is an invaluable resource for LLC leaders. Keeping up with the latest legal developments and business strategies ensures that your LLC remains competitive and compliant. Consider enrolling in courses that focus on business law and management. Many educational institutions offer online courses tailored to busy professionals, allowing you to learn at your own pace. Webinars on legal updates are another excellent resource. These sessions often feature experts who provide insights into recent changes in the law and how they might impact your business. Staying informed through these educational avenues equips you with the knowledge to make sound decisions and adapt to the ever-changing legal environment.

To further support your LLC's legal needs, utilizing templates and checklists can simplify document preparation and compliance tracking. Access to sample contracts and agreements provides a foundation for drafting legally sound documents tailored to your business needs. These templates serve as a starting point, ensuring that all critical elements are included and reducing the risk of errors. These templates can be supplied by your lawyer as a starting point to any contract or document preparation. Compliance checklists are equally beneficial, offering a clear overview of your legal obligations and helping you track your progress. By systematically working through these checklists, you can ensure that all necessary steps are completed, reducing the likelihood of compliance issues arising. These resources not only save time but also provide peace of mind, knowing that your LLC is adhering to legal requirements. These checklists would be available on your state's website.

Joining legal associations or networks can provide significant advantages for your LLC. These memberships offer access to expert advice and the opportunity to consult with professionals who specialize in business law. Engaging with these experts allows you to gain insights into complex legal matters and ensures that your LLC receives the guidance needed to navigate legal challenges. Additionally, these associations often host networking events, providing opportunities to connect with other business owners and legal professionals. Building a network of contacts within these circles can lead to valuable collaborations and partnerships, as well as offering a support system when legal questions arise. The relationships forged through these memberships can be instrumental in your LLC's success, providing resources and connections that are otherwise difficult to obtain.

As we conclude this chapter on maintaining legal compliance and utilizing resources, it's clear that a proactive approach is key. By leveraging tools, staying educated, and building networks, you lay a strong foundation for your LLC's success. These strategies not only ensure compliance but also empower you to navigate the complexities of the business world with confidence. With these systems in place, you're well-prepared to face the challenges of running an LLC, knowing you have the support and resources needed to thrive.

Don't move on to the next chapter without doing the following;

1. Add key compliance dates into your diary as well as a reminder a couple of weeks before to get started
2. Is your business big enough to have a compliance officer? Who would be that for your LLC?
3. Are you happy with your operating agreement? Does any of it need re-drafting to be more fit for purpose?
4. Do you need to subscribe to local legal bulletins to keep up to date with legislation changes? Or subscribe to useful webinars?

Chapter 5

Expanding and Scaling Your LLC

This chapter moves away from the theoretical nature of setting up and running your LLC, to how does your business grow. It may not have been what you expected when picking up this book, but if you're not growing, you're going backwards.

Picture this: your business is thriving, and you're considering taking the next big step to expand. The prospect of scaling your LLC is both exciting and daunting, filled with opportunities and potential pitfalls. Growth requires a strategic approach, one that aligns with your business model and market demands. As you ponder the path forward, imagine yourself standing at the helm of a ship, ready to navigate the seas of expansion with confidence and clarity. This chapter is your compass, guiding you through the essential strategies for scaling your LLC successfully.

Identifying a scalable business model is the first step in this journey. Not all business models lend themselves to easy scaling, so it's crucial to choose one that does. Subscription services, for instance, offer a predictable revenue stream that grows with your customer base. Consider businesses like Netflix, which have capitalized on the subscription model to achieve massive growth. This approach provides a stable foundation for expansion, allowing you to forecast revenue and plan accordingly. Franchising is another avenue to explore, offering a way to replicate your successful business model in new locations. By licensing your brand and business practices, you can expand rapidly without bearing the full cost of each new location. This model has been the backbone of many successful chains, enabling them to grow quickly while maintaining quality and consistency.

Optimizing operational efficiencies is another crucial aspect of scaling. As demand increases, your operations must adapt to handle the added pressure. Lean management principles can streamline processes, eliminating waste and increasing efficiency. This approach focuses on delivering maximum value with minimal resources, ensuring that every part of your operation is as efficient as possible. Implementing quality control systems is equally important, ensuring that your products or services meet high standards even as you scale. By maintaining quality and consistency, you build trust with your customers, encouraging repeat business and fostering loyalty.

Financing growth is often necessary when scaling your LLC, and exploring various funding options is key. Venture capital is a popular choice for businesses with high growth potential, providing significant funds in exchange for equity. This influx of capital can accelerate expansion, allowing you to invest in new markets, hire additional staff, or develop new products. However, securing venture capital requires a compelling business plan and a clear vision for growth. Small business loans and grants are also viable options, offering a more traditional route to financing. These funds can support expansion efforts without diluting ownership, providing the resources needed to scale effectively.

Developing a comprehensive growth plan is essential to guide your expansion efforts. Start by setting measurable growth targets, outlining specific goals for your business over a defined period. These targets should be ambitious yet achievable, providing a road map for your scaling efforts. Conducting a SWOT analysis can help identify strengths, weaknesses, opportunities, and threats, providing a clear picture of your business's position in the market. This analysis informs strategic decisions, highlighting areas for improvement and potential risks. By understanding your business's current state and future potential, you can craft a plan that aligns with your vision for growth.

Reflection Section: Crafting Your Growth Strategy

Consider your current business model and how it aligns with your scaling goals. Reflect on the potential for subscription services or franchising in your industry. Assess your operational efficiencies and identify areas for improvement. Explore financing options that align with your growth strategy, and draft a preliminary growth plan with measurable targets. Use this reflection to inform your next steps in scaling your LLC.

Scaling your LLC is a complex yet rewarding endeavor. By identifying scalable models, optimizing operations, securing funding, and developing a strategic growth plan, you position your business for success in a competitive market.

5.1 Exploring New Markets and Opportunities

Venturing into new markets requires a keen understanding of the landscape you're entering. Conducting thorough market research is your first step. This involves analyzing competitor landscapes to see who the players are and what they're offering. By understanding their strengths and weaknesses, you can identify gaps your business might fill. It's also crucial to know your customer demographics. Who are your potential customers in this new market? What are their preferences and buying habits? This information is invaluable. It helps tailor your products or services to meet the specific needs of your target audience, ensuring that your business resonates with them.

Once you've gathered the necessary insights, it's time to evaluate your market entry strategies. One approach is forming strategic partnerships. These alliances can provide local knowledge and resources, reducing the risks associated with entering unfamiliar territory. A partnership with a local firm can offer immediate credibility and access to established networks. Alternatively, direct investment involves setting up your operations from scratch, giving you full control but also requiring more resources and commitment.

Licensing and franchising offer another route, allowing you to expand your brand without the overhead of managing new locations directly. This approach leverages local entrepreneurs who understand the market nuances and can operate under your brand's established reputation.

As you weigh these strategies, it's important to assess the risks and rewards of expanding into new territories. Regulatory hurdles are a significant consideration. Different regions may have varying laws and regulations that could impact your operations. Compliance is key, and understanding these regulations beforehand can save you from legal headaches later. On the other hand, the potential for increased revenue is a powerful motivator. A successful expansion can open doors to new revenue streams and customer bases, significantly boosting your business's growth trajectory. However, it's essential to balance these potential gains with an awareness of the challenges that come with operating in unfamiliar markets. Ensure you get independent legal advice here so you can assess what you're doing to protect your existing business from too much risk. You may need CPA advice here too, but a lawyer can advise on whether your current LLC and operating agreement are sufficient.

To succeed in new markets, adapting your marketing strategies to appeal to local audiences is crucial. Culturally relevant advertising can make a significant difference in how your brand is perceived. Understanding cultural nuances and preferences allows you to craft messages that resonate with local consumers. This might involve translating marketing materials into the local language or incorporating cultural symbols and references that hold meaning for your audience. Localization of product offerings is another strategy to consider. This means tailoring your products or services to meet the specific needs and preferences of the local market. It might involve modifying product features, pricing, or packaging to align with local tastes and purchasing power.

As you explore these new opportunities, it's essential to stay agile and responsive to the insights you gather. The business landscape is ever-changing, and being able to pivot based on real-time data and feedback is a valuable asset. This adaptability ensures that your expansion efforts remain aligned with market demands, allowing you to seize opportunities as they arise. By conducting thorough research, evaluating entry strategies, assessing risks and rewards, and adapting your marketing efforts, you position your business for success in new markets.

5.2 Hiring and Managing Employees within an LLC

As your LLC begins to expand, the need to hire employees becomes inevitable. Crafting a robust hiring strategy is critical to attracting and retaining top talent. It starts with building a strong employer brand. A compelling employer brand not only attracts candidates but also sets expectations about your company culture and values. Think about what makes your LLC unique and how you can communicate that to potential employees. Your brand should resonate across your recruitment materials, from your website to your job postings. Utilizing recruitment platforms like LinkedIn, Indeed, or specialized industry sites can widen your reach, bringing your job openings to the attention of a diverse pool of candidates. These platforms allow you to target your search, ensuring that your job listings reach qualified candidates who align with your company's values and objectives.

Once you've attracted the right candidates, effective HR policies become the backbone of a growing workforce. Establishing a comprehensive employee handbook is a pivotal step. This document sets the tone for your workplace, outlining expectations, procedures, and benefits. It serves as a reference point for employees and management alike, ensuring consistency in handling various situations. Performance evaluation processes are equally important. Regular reviews provide employees with feedback, helping them understand their strengths and areas for improvement. They also offer a platform for setting goals and aligning individual performance with company objectives. A well-structured evaluation process can motivate employees, fostering a culture of continuous improvement and contribution. These processes can also help protect you if things go wrong with employees and you have to potentially let people go.

Fostering a positive company culture is essential in maintaining a motivated and productive workforce. Team-building activities are a powerful tool in this regard. Whether it's a company retreat, a quarterly outing, or a simple team lunch, these activities break down barriers and encourage collaboration. They help build relationships and trust among team members, creating a more cohesive and supportive work environment. Open communication channels further enhance this environment. Encourage transparency and feedback, allowing employees to voice their opinions and ideas without fear of reprisal. Regular team meetings and one-on-one check-ins can facilitate this open dialogue, ensuring that everyone feels heard and valued.

In today's dynamic work environment, offering flexible work arrangements can be a significant advantage in attracting diverse talent. Remote work policies, for instance, can widen your talent pool beyond geographical constraints, allowing you to hire the best candidates regardless of location. Establish clear guidelines and expectations to ensure remote work remains productive and in alignment with business goals. Flexible scheduling options also cater to employees seeking a better work-life balance. Allowing employees to adjust their work hours to better suit their personal lives can lead to increased job satisfaction and retention. It demonstrates a commitment to employee well-being, which is increasingly important in today's competitive job market.

As you navigate the complexities of hiring and managing employees within your LLC, remember that the foundation of a successful team lies in clear communication and mutual respect. Each new hire is an investment in your company's future, bringing fresh ideas and energy. By cultivating a supportive and inclusive work environment, you empower your employees to thrive, contributing to the overall success and growth of your LLC.

5.3 Incorporating Technological Solutions for Growth

In today's fast-paced business landscape, technology acts as a catalyst for growth, offering tools that streamline operations and enhance efficiency.

Automation stands at the forefront, allowing you to offload routine tasks and focus on core activities. Imagine automating your email marketing campaigns or using software to reconcile your accounts. These tools eliminate repetitive manual work, reducing errors and freeing up time for strategic planning. This shift from manual to automated processes can transform your day-to-day operations, making them more efficient and less labor-intensive. The use of cloud-based collaboration tools further enhances operational efficiency. Platforms like Slack or Microsoft Teams facilitate seamless communication among team members, regardless of their location. These tools foster a collaborative environment, ensuring that everyone stays aligned with the company's goals and objectives. They also provide a centralized hub for sharing documents and ideas, encouraging innovation and real-time problem-solving.

Implementing a customer relationship management (CRM) system can revolutionize how you interact with your clients. By providing a comprehensive view of customer interactions, a CRM allows you to offer personalized services that enhance customer satisfaction. Imagine having access to a customer's history, allowing you to tailor your communications and offers specifically to them. This level of personalization builds loyalty and trust, fostering long-term relationships. Additionally, CRM systems provide data-driven insights that inform your sales strategies. With access to detailed analytics, you can identify trends and patterns, enabling you to make informed decisions that drive sales and growth. These systems also help you manage your sales pipeline, ensuring that no opportunities are missed and that each lead is nurtured effectively.

The potential of e-commerce to expand your reach cannot be overstated. Establishing an online storefront opens your business to a global audience, removing geographical limitations. Whether you're selling handmade crafts or digital products, an online presence can significantly boost your sales and visibility. E-commerce platforms like Shopify or WooCommerce simplify the process, offering templates and tools that make it easy to set up and manage your store. Integrating digital payment solutions is another critical component, providing customers with a seamless and secure transaction experience. Options like PayPal, Apple Pay, or credit card processing not only enhance convenience but also build trust with your customers, encouraging repeat business and positive word-of-mouth.

Leveraging data analytics for strategic decision-making is a powerful way to refine your business strategies. Predictive analytics, for instance, can forecast market trends, allowing you to stay ahead of the competition. By analyzing historical data, you can anticipate customer needs and adjust your offerings accordingly. This proactive approach ensures that your business remains relevant and competitive in a constantly evolving market. Additionally, customer behavior analysis provides insights into buying patterns and preferences. By understanding what drives your customers' decisions, you can tailor your marketing efforts to better meet their needs. These analytics offer a data-driven foundation for strategic planning, ensuring that your decisions are informed and aligned with your business objectives.

5.4 Building Strategic Partnerships and Collaborations

In the world of business, strategic partnerships can be a powerful catalyst for growth and innovation. Identifying potential partners involves more than just finding a company with a good reputation. It's about aligning your goals and values with those of another organization to create a mutually beneficial relationship. Start by looking for businesses with complementary product offerings. For instance, if your LLC specializes in graphic design, partnering with a printing company could enhance your service portfolio. Together, you can offer clients a seamless experience from design to print, expanding your reach and adding value to your services. Additionally, consider partners who share a similar target audience. This alignment ensures that your marketing efforts are cohesive and that both parties benefit from the collaboration. When your audiences overlap, co-marketing campaigns become more effective, driving engagement and sales for both businesses involved.

Once you've identified potential partners, the next step is negotiating collaboration agreements. These agreements lay the foundation for a successful partnership by clearly defining roles and responsibilities. It's crucial to ensure that each party understands what they're bringing to the table and what they can expect in return. This clarity prevents misunderstandings and fosters a sense of trust and cooperation. Profit-sharing arrangements should also be discussed and agreed upon up front to avoid conflicts down the line. Whether you decide on a fixed percentage or a more flexible arrangement, transparency is key. Open and honest communication about financial expectations sets the tone for a partnership built on mutual respect and shared goals.

Leveraging partnerships for mutual growth is where the true potential of collaboration lies. Co-marketing campaigns, for example, allow you to pool resources and reach a wider audience than you could alone. By combining your marketing efforts, you can create impactful campaigns that resonate with your shared target audience. Joint product development is another avenue to explore. When two companies come together to create a new product, they bring diverse perspectives and expertise to the table, resulting in innovative solutions that might not have been possible individually. This collaborative innovation can lead to unique offerings that set you apart in the marketplace, driving growth and attracting new customers.

Evaluating partnership performance is an ongoing process that ensures your collaborations remain beneficial and aligned with your goals. Setting Key Performance Indicators (KPIs) for each partnership is a practical way to measure success. These metrics might include sales growth, customer acquisition, or brand visibility. Regular performance reviews allow you to assess whether the partnership is meeting its objectives and where improvements can be made. These evaluations provide an opportunity to recalibrate the partnership if necessary, ensuring it continues to deliver value to both parties. By maintaining open lines of communication and regularly assessing performance, you can adapt to changing circumstances and maximize the benefits of your strategic alliances.

5.5 Preparing for Future Business Challenges

Running a business means always being ready for the unexpected. Market conditions can shift rapidly, and staying ahead of these changes is crucial for sustaining success. One effective strategy is diversifying your revenue streams. By not relying solely on one source of income, you protect your business from the impact of market fluctuations. Consider adding new products or services that complement your existing offerings. This not only spreads risk but also opens up new opportunities for growth. For instance, a publishing company might expand into digital content or online courses, tapping into different customer needs and preferences.

Scenario planning is another valuable tool. By envisioning various future events and developing potential responses, you prepare your business for a range of possibilities. This proactive approach allows you to adapt quickly, whether facing economic downturns or sudden industry shifts. Create "what-if" scenarios to explore how different factors could influence your business. By doing this, you can develop flexible strategies and make informed decisions that keep your company resilient in the face of change.

A robust risk management plan is also vital. Begin by assessing your current insurance coverage. Ensure it aligns with your business's risks and needs. Insurance can safeguard against unforeseen events, providing financial stability. Review your policies regularly and adjust them as your business evolves. Additionally, establish crisis management protocols. These guidelines should outline steps to take during emergencies, ensuring a coordinated response. This might include communication strategies, resource allocation, and roles for team members. Being prepared minimizes disruption and helps maintain customer trust.

Keeping abreast of industry trends is equally important. Attending industry conferences provides insights into emerging developments and innovations. These events offer a platform to connect with peers, exchange ideas, and gain inspiration. Subscribing to trade publications is another way to stay informed. These resources deliver up-to-date news, analysis, and expert opinions, equipping you with the knowledge needed to navigate changes. By understanding the latest trends, you position your business to capitalize on new opportunities and avoid pitfalls.

Fostering a culture of continuous innovation within your organization is a powerful way to maintain competitiveness. Encourage employee creativity by creating an environment where new ideas are welcomed and explored. This could involve regular brainstorming sessions or dedicated time for innovation projects. Recognize and reward creative contributions, motivating your team to think outside the box. Investing in research and development is another avenue to explore. By dedicating resources to R&D, you drive innovation and enhance your offerings. This commitment to innovation keeps your business at the forefront of your industry, setting you apart from competitors and attracting customers seeking the latest advancements.

In preparing for future business challenges, you build a foundation for long-term success. Diversifying revenue streams, planning for scenarios, managing risks, and embracing innovation are all part of this strategy. By staying informed and agile, you navigate change with confidence, ensuring your business remains robust and adaptable. This proactive approach not only safeguards your company but also positions it to thrive in an ever-evolving landscape.

Don't move on to the next chapter without doing the following;

1. Do you have a growth plan for your business? Does this include revenue projections and expanding your staff as you grow? Do you need to investigate different funding models for your growth?
2. If you are planning to grow, do you have targeted specific products or geographies? Take this to the next level and list some potential collaborations with other businesses that could work, and reach out to them when the time is right

Chapter 6

Advanced LLC Strategies and Considerations

Imagine standing at the crossroads of business growth, where the path you choose could significantly impact your financial landscape. Electing S-Corp status for your LLC is one such decision that holds the potential to redefine your tax responsibilities and operational dynamics. While the LLC structure offers flexibility and protection, converting to an S-Corp could unlock specific benefits, especially regarding taxation. This chapter will guide you through the intricacies of making this strategic shift, offering insights into whether it aligns with your business goals and circumstances.

Converting your LLC to an S-Corp primarily revolves around the allure of tax savings. At the core of this appeal lies the ability to avoid self-employment tax on distributions. Typically, LLC owners are subject to self-employment tax on the entire business income, encompassing both their salary and any additional profits. By electing S-Corp status, you separate your income into two streams: a reasonable salary and distributions. While the salary remains subject to payroll taxes, the distributions are taxed as personal income, exempt from self-employment tax. This split can result in significant tax savings, allowing you to retain more of your hard-earned profits for reinvestment or personal use. Additionally, the operational flexibility of an S-Corp can streamline your financial planning, providing a balanced approach to compensation and profit allocation.

However, before you embark on this path, it's crucial to assess your eligibility for S-Corp status. Not every LLC qualifies, and understanding the criteria is essential. First and foremost, your LLC must be a domestic entity, ensuring it operates within the United States. The shareholder count is another critical factor; an S-Corp is limited to 100 shareholders, which can include individuals, certain trusts, and estates, but not corporations or partnerships. Moreover, all shareholders must be U.S. citizens or residents—a restriction that could impact businesses with international partners. Finally, an S-Corp can only issue one class of stock, which means all shares must confer identical rights to dividends and liquidation proceeds. These requirements ensure that the S-Corp structure remains streamlined and straightforward, aligning with its intended purpose of benefiting small to medium-sized businesses.

Once you've determined your eligibility, the conversion process involves specific steps. The first is to file IRS Form 2553, formally requesting S-Corp status for tax purposes. This form must be submitted within two months and 15 days after the start of your tax year to apply for the current year. While the process might seem straightforward, it's wise to consult with a tax professional to ensure compliance and address any complexities unique to your situation. It's important to remember that this election is for federal tax purposes and doesn't alter your LLC's legal structure at the state level. Therefore, you should also review any state-specific considerations, as some states impose different tax rules on S-Corps that could affect your decision.

Despite the potential benefits, converting to an S-Corp isn't without its drawbacks. One of the most notable challenges is the increased complexity in tax filings. As an S-Corp, you must maintain meticulous payroll records and ensure that the owners receive a reasonable salary. Failure to adhere to these requirements can lead to penalties and even the revocation of your S-Corp status by the IRS. Additionally, the restriction to a single class of stock may limit your ability to implement complex equity arrangements or attract diverse investors. These limitations could be significant depending on your business's growth strategy and funding needs. While the tax advantages can be appealing, it's vital to weigh these potential limitations against your business objectives and operational capacity.

Reflection Section: Is S-Corp Status Right for Your LLC?

Consider your current business structure and financial goals. Reflect on whether the tax savings and operational benefits of an S-Corp align with your objectives. Evaluate your eligibility based on shareholder composition and state-specific considerations. Consult with a tax professional to explore the feasibility and implications of conversion. Use this reflection to determine if the S-Corp path will enhance your business strategy.

6.1 Utilizing Asset Protection Strategies

As a business owner, the thought of protecting your personal and business assets is likely never far from your mind. Developing robust asset protection strategies is not just a precaution; it's a vital part of sustaining your business's health and your peace of mind. One effective method is creating multiple LLCs to segregate assets. This approach is particularly useful if you run several distinct business operations or own multiple properties. By placing each venture or asset under a separate LLC, you limit liability exposure. If one LLC faces legal trouble, your other assets remain insulated, like compartments on a ship preventing a single leak from sinking it. This strategy requires careful planning and compliance with state laws, but it can be a powerful tool for risk management.

Trusts offer another layer of asset protection worth considering. An irrevocable trust, for instance, transfers ownership of assets out of your name, making them inaccessible to creditors. Because you relinquish control over the assets placed in an irrevocable trust, they are no longer considered part of your estate, shielding them from personal liability claims. Additionally, land trusts can be employed specifically for real estate holdings. These trusts can obscure property ownership from public records, providing privacy and protection against legal claims. While trusts can be complex to set up, consulting with a legal professional can ensure they're structured to maximize protection and align with your financial goals. When you consult with a legal professional, talk to them about your long-term goals for the business, not just your 12-month plans, as they may change their advice based on your long-term view of where you want the business to go.

Understanding the legal protections available to LLCs is crucial in fortifying your defense against liabilities. One such mechanism is charging order protection. In the event that a creditor wins a judgment against an LLC member, a charging order limits the creditor's reach to the member's distribution rights, rather than the LLC's assets themselves. This protection maintains the integrity of the business while fulfilling legal obligations to creditors. However, to fully benefit from these protections, maintaining corporate formalities is essential. This means keeping personal and business finances separate, holding regular meetings if required, and adhering to the terms set forth in your operating agreement. By treating your LLC as a separate legal entity, you reinforce its protective barrier against personal liabilities.

Insurance stands as a cornerstone in any comprehensive asset protection plan. Professional liability insurance is especially important for those providing services or advice, guarding against claims of negligence or malpractice. This type of insurance covers legal costs and settlements, ensuring that a single lawsuit doesn't cripple your business. Umbrella insurance policies offer additional coverage that extends beyond the limits of your standard policies. These policies provide a safety net, covering unexpected incidents and liabilities that surpass typical insurance limits. Both types of insurance are investments in your business's stability, offering reassurance that you're protected against unforeseen challenges.

Asset protection is not a one-size-fits-all solution, but rather a tailored strategy that evolves with your business. As you grow and expand, your needs will change, and your protection strategies should adapt accordingly. By employing a combination of LLC structures, trusts, legal mechanisms, and insurance, you create a resilient shield around your assets, allowing you to focus on growing your business with confidence. This proactive approach to asset protection not only guards against liabilities but also provides the peace of mind necessary to lead with assurance. Whether you're a sole trader, freelancer, or a business owner with a diverse portfolio, these strategies offer a comprehensive framework to secure your financial future amidst the unpredictable terrain of entrepreneurship.

6.2 Implementing Advanced Tax Strategies

Navigating the complex world of taxes can feel like a daunting task, but implementing advanced tax strategies can significantly lighten your financial burden. One such approach is income splitting, a technique that involves distributing income across multiple entities or individuals to minimize overall tax liability. For business owners, employing family members can be an effective method. By hiring a spouse or child to work in your business, you can shift income to them, potentially placing them in a lower tax bracket and reducing your family's total tax obligation. Additionally, consider dividend income strategies within your LLC. By paying yourself dividends instead of a salary, you can lower your exposure to payroll taxes, though this requires careful planning to ensure compliance with tax regulations.

Tax deferral opportunities offer another avenue for strategic financial planning. Contributing to retirement plans, like a SEP IRA or a Solo 401(k), not only prepares you for the future but also allows you to defer taxes on the contributed income. This deferred tax can be particularly advantageous if you anticipate being in a lower tax bracket upon retirement. Similarly, like-kind exchanges, particularly in real estate, allow you to defer capital gains taxes by reinvesting proceeds from a sold property into a similar property. This strategy can be a powerful tool for real estate investors looking to expand or upgrade their portfolios while postponing the tax hit.

Leveraging tax credits and incentives can further enhance your tax savings. Research and development (R&D) tax credits are available for businesses investing in innovation and improvements. If your company is creating new products or processes, these credits can offset some of the costs, effectively lowering your taxable income. Additionally, energy efficiency incentives are offered to businesses that implement eco-friendly practices. Whether you're upgrading to energy-efficient lighting or installing solar panels, these incentives not only reduce your environmental footprint but also your tax bill. By staying informed about available credits, you ensure your business capitalizes on every opportunity to save.

Planning for tax-efficient exits is crucial for business owners contemplating a sale or transition. Installment sales allow you to receive payments over time, spreading the tax liability across several years rather than incurring it all at once. This method can ease the tax burden and provide a steady income stream post-sale. Structured buyouts offer another strategic option, particularly when selling to an internal party, such as a business partner. By structuring the buyout over time, you can align the tax impact with your financial goals. These strategies require careful consideration and planning to ensure they align with both your immediate needs and long-term financial aspirations.

Implementing these advanced tax strategies requires diligence and often the expertise of a tax professional. However, the benefits they offer in terms of reducing liabilities and enhancing financial planning are substantial. For business people, sole traders, freelancers, and publishers, these strategies can mean the difference between a stressful tax season and one that aligns with their broader financial goals. By exploring these avenues, you not only manage your current tax obligations more effectively but also position your business for sustainable growth and success in the years to come.

6.3 Leveraging LLCs for Real Estate Investments

Investing in real estate can be an exciting opportunity for growth and income, yet it also comes with its fair share of risks. Choosing to operate under an LLC offers distinct advantages for property investors, making it a popular choice for those looking to shield personal assets from potential liabilities. The primary benefit of using an LLC for real estate ventures is liability protection. When you own property through an LLC, your personal assets remain separate from business debts or legal issues that may arise from property ownership. This separation means that if a tenant sues your business due to an incident on the property, your personal savings, home, and other assets are not at risk. This peace of mind allows you to focus on maximizing your investment returns without the constant worry of personal financial exposure. I would suggest creating a separate LLC for real estate that is different from the LLC you conduct your business from so that you protect the liability of each LLC independently.

In addition to liability protection, LLCs offer the advantage of pass-through taxation on rental income. Unlike corporations, which face double taxation on profits, LLCs allow income to flow directly to the owners, who then report it on their personal tax returns. This means you only pay taxes once, potentially saving you a significant amount of money that can be reinvested into expanding your property portfolio. This tax structure can be particularly beneficial for real estate investors who rely on rental income as a primary revenue stream. By minimizing the tax burden, you can enhance your cash flow, enabling you to manage and grow your investments more effectively.

Securing financing for real estate investments also becomes more accessible with an LLC. Lenders often view LLCs as more professional and stable than individual investors, which can improve your chances of securing favorable loan terms. Commercial real estate loans are tailored for such entities, offering larger amounts and longer repayment terms compared to residential mortgages. These loans are designed to support the purchase of income-generating properties, providing the capital needed to acquire and develop commercial real estate. Alternatively, hard money lenders offer short-term loans secured by the real property itself, which can be useful for investors looking to flip properties or undertake renovations. These lenders focus more on the property's value rather than the borrower's credit, offering flexibility for those with varying financial backgrounds.

Efficient property management is crucial for maintaining and enhancing the value of your real estate investments. Hiring a professional property management company can alleviate the daily burdens of managing properties, such as handling tenant issues, maintenance requests, and rent collection. These companies bring expertise and resources that ensure your properties are well-maintained and your tenants are satisfied, which can reduce turnover and increase profitability. Additionally, implementing thorough tenant screening processes is vital. By conducting background checks and verifying employment and rental history, you can minimize the risk of problematic tenants, safeguarding your investment from potential legal issues and financial losses. Proper management practices not only preserve the value of your properties but also contribute to a stable and predictable income stream.

When structuring real estate deals, careful planning is key to optimizing returns and protecting your interests. Joint ventures in real estate are a common strategy, allowing you to partner with other investors or developers who bring complementary skills or resources to the table. These partnerships can provide the financial backing or expertise needed to undertake larger or more complex projects. By clearly defining roles, responsibilities, and profit-sharing arrangements in a joint venture agreement, you ensure that all parties are aligned and committed to the project's success. Another approach is syndication, where you pool funds from multiple investors to acquire a property. This method allows you to access larger investments without bearing the entire financial burden yourself, diversifying your risk across multiple stakeholders. Syndication requires careful legal structuring to comply with securities regulations, but it can be an effective way to expand your real estate portfolio and achieve higher returns.

Real estate investments present a diverse range of opportunities, and leveraging the advantages of an LLC can significantly enhance your ability to capitalize on them. By understanding the benefits of liability protection, tax efficiencies, and strategic partnerships, you position yourself to navigate the complexities of real estate with confidence. Whether you're acquiring your first rental property or expanding into commercial real estate, the right strategies and structures can make all the difference in your success.

6.4 Navigating Multi-Member LLC Dynamics

In the realm of multi-member LLCs, maintaining healthy relationships among members isn't just good practice—it's a necessity. Picture your LLC as a finely tuned orchestra, where each member plays a distinct instrument. Regular communication is the conductor that keeps all the musicians in harmony. Establishing open and consistent channels—whether through scheduled meetings, collaborative platforms, or casual check-ins—ensures that everyone remains on the same page. This regularity fosters transparency and trust, promoting a culture where members feel valued and heard. Moreover, clearly defined roles and responsibilities within the LLC act as sheet music, guiding each member in their unique contributions. By delineating tasks and expectations, you reduce misunderstandings and enhance efficiency, allowing each member to focus on their strengths while contributing to the collective success of the LLC.

Decision-making in a multi-member LLC can sometimes feel like navigating a ship through turbulent waters. The key is having a clear and structured process, akin to a reliable compass. Voting procedures, often outlined in the LLC's Operating Agreement, serve as the foundation for making decisions that affect the group. These procedures might require a simple majority for routine matters but necessitate a super majority for significant changes, ensuring that all voices are considered. Additionally, forming committees to handle specific decisions can streamline the process, leveraging the expertise of certain members for specialized tasks. This not only expedites decision-making but also empowers members by tapping into their individual strengths and interests, fostering a sense of ownership and commitment to the LLC's objectives.

Conflicts among members are inevitable, much like occasional storms at sea. However, having a robust conflict resolution strategy is akin to having a sturdy lifeboat, ready to navigate choppy waters. Incorporating mediation and arbitration clauses into your Operating Agreement provides a structured process for addressing disputes. Mediation allows for facilitated negotiation, encouraging members to find mutually agreeable solutions, while arbitration offers a more formal resolution, often binding. Additionally, training members in conflict resolution can equip them with valuable skills to address issues constructively, preventing minor disagreements from escalating into larger problems. By fostering an environment where conflicts are addressed openly and respectfully, you maintain a harmonious and productive atmosphere within your LLC.

Changes in membership, whether through additions, exits, or transfers, are as natural as the ebb and flow of tides. Planning for these transitions involves clear processes and agreements, much like having a map to guide your journey. Buy-sell agreements are critical tools in this regard, outlining the terms under which a member can sell their interest in the LLC. These agreements specify who can buy the departing member's interest and at what price, ensuring a smooth transition that minimizes disruption. Additionally, conducting thorough membership interest valuations helps establish a fair market value for the departing member's stake, preventing disputes and ensuring equitable treatment for all parties involved. By addressing these potential changes proactively, you create a stable and resilient LLC that can adapt to evolving circumstances while maintaining its core integrity and mission.

Navigating the dynamics of a multi-member LLC requires a delicate balance of communication, structure, and foresight. By fostering open dialogue, establishing clear decision-making processes, equipping members with conflict resolution skills, and planning for membership changes, you create an environment of collaboration and mutual respect. This approach not only strengthens the internal fabric of your LLC but also positions it for sustainable growth and success in the ever-changing business landscape. As you continue to navigate these dynamics, remember that each member's unique contributions and perspectives are invaluable assets, enriching your LLC's journey and propelling it toward future achievements.

6.5 Exiting or Dissolving Your LLC – Key Considerations

Thinking about leaving your LLC involves a lot of planning and strategic decision-making. For many, selling the business to a third party is a viable option. This route allows you to transfer ownership while potentially realizing a substantial financial gain. It often involves valuing your business accurately, marketing it to potential buyers, and negotiating terms that meet your objectives. The process requires patience and due diligence, ensuring that the buyer aligns with your business values and vision. Another exit strategy is merging with another company. This pathway can offer synergies that enhance value for both parties involved. Merging might mean combining resources, expanding market presence, or diversifying offerings. It's essential to conduct thorough evaluations to ensure compatibility between the companies before proceeding with a merger. Both these strategies can provide a smooth transition while maximizing the benefits of your hard work.

Understanding the formal dissolution process is crucial if you decide that winding down is the best course of action. Legally dissolving an LLC involves several steps, starting with filing dissolution paperwork with the state. This official documentation notifies the state of your intent to cease operations, removing your business from the state's records. Once the paperwork is filed, settling outstanding debts and obligations becomes a priority. This includes paying off creditors, closing accounts, and distributing any remaining assets among the members. Properly closing these financial loops ensures that you exit with a clean slate, free from lingering liabilities. It's also wise to cancel any permits or licenses associated with your business to prevent future complications.

Navigating the tax implications of exiting or dissolving an LLC is another layer of complexity. Selling your business may lead to capital gains tax on the sale proceeds. This tax is assessed based on the profit from the sale, calculated by subtracting your original investment from the final selling price. Understanding how this tax functions helps you plan effectively, potentially minimizing your tax liability through strategic planning. Additionally, handling final tax returns is a necessary step to officially close your business's financial records. Filing these returns accurately ensures compliance and avoids potential penalties. Engaging with a tax professional can provide clarity and guidance throughout this process, ensuring that all obligations are met.

Ensuring business continuity when a key member exits is vital for maintaining stability. Succession planning plays a pivotal role in this process, identifying potential successors and preparing them for leadership roles. This foresight ensures that the business continues to operate smoothly, even in the absence of a key figure. Transitioning client relationships is equally important. Clients may feel uncertain about changes in leadership, so it's crucial to communicate transparently and reassure them of your ongoing commitment to quality and service. Building strong relationships with clients and stakeholders can ease transitions, maintaining trust and loyalty throughout the process.

As we conclude this chapter, remember that exiting or dissolving your LLC doesn't signal an end but a transformation. Whether selling, merging, or winding down, each path offers opportunities for growth and evolution. As you consider these options, ensure that your decisions align with your broader vision and future aspirations. With careful planning and strategic execution, you can navigate these transitions with confidence, setting the stage for future endeavors. In the next chapter, we will explore industry-specific guidance, offering insights to further tailor your strategies to your unique business landscape.

Don't move on to the next chapter without doing the following;

1. Does any of this content resonate with you that you need to engage legal or tax help? The initial creation of an LLC is the easy part; it is all the ongoing nuances that have more complexity

Chapter 7

Industry-Specific Guidance for LLCs

Imagine a world where your creative genius is not just recognized but also protected. As a freelancer or creative professional, your work is your livelihood. It's your art, your voice, and sometimes, your lifeline. Yet, the very nature of freelancing can leave you vulnerable to risks that threaten both your personal and professional life. This is where forming an LLC can be transformative. By establishing an LLC, you not only elevate your professional image but also safeguard your personal assets from potential legal battles or financial disputes. This structure acts as a protective barrier, ensuring that your creativity flourishes without the looming fear of personal liability.

The benefits of forming an LLC extend beyond mere protection. As a freelancer, your credibility is your currency. An LLC enhances your professional standing, signaling to clients that you are a serious business entity. This perception can open doors to new opportunities, attract higher-paying clients, and secure long-term contracts. It's a declaration of your commitment to your craft, elevating your status from a mere freelancer to a professional service provider. It's this elevation that can set you apart in a crowded marketplace, allowing you to command respect and negotiate from a position of strength.

Tax considerations are another critical aspect where an LLC can offer significant advantages. Freelancers often face the challenge of fluctuating income and complex tax obligations. An LLC provides a flexible framework that can be tailored to optimize tax efficiency. You can deduct legitimate business expenses, reducing your taxable income and freeing up resources for reinvestment or personal savings. Managing self-employment taxes becomes more straightforward, with options to treat your LLC as a sole proprietorship or elect S Corp status for potential tax savings. This flexibility empowers you to craft a tax strategy that aligns with your financial goals, minimizing liabilities while maximizing benefits.

Navigating client contracts is a vital skill for freelancers, and an LLC can provide the foundation for solid contract management. Standard contract templates, tailored to your industry, ensure that your agreements are comprehensive and legally sound. These templates can be customized to define project scopes, payment terms, and deliverables, providing clarity and protection for both parties. Negotiating contract terms becomes a strategic exercise, allowing you to assert your value while safeguarding your interests. With the backing of an LLC, you can approach contract negotiations with confidence, knowing that your business has the legal framework to support and enforce your agreements.

Intellectual property is often the lifeblood of creative professionals. Protecting your creative works through an LLC is an investment in your future. Copyright registration processes can be streamlined under an LLC, ensuring that your creations are legally protected from unauthorized use. Licensing agreements become more manageable, allowing you to monetize your work while retaining control over how it's used. This protection extends beyond legal safeguards, giving you peace of mind to focus on innovation and creativity. In a world where intellectual property is a valuable asset, an LLC provides the tools to protect, manage, and leverage your creations effectively.

Reflection Section: Assess Your Current Structure

Take a moment to consider your current business structure. Are you operating as a sole proprietor, and are your assets adequately protected? Reflect on how forming an LLC could enhance your professional image, streamline your tax obligations, and safeguard your intellectual property. Consider jotting down any questions you have about the process and use this guide as a resource to explore the potential benefits of an LLC for your freelance business. Whilst there are tax savings as an LLC, the primary benefit I see is asset protection and perception from customers and others that you are more legitimate as an LLC.

7.1 Publishing Industry Insights for LLC Owners

In the expansive world of publishing, the structure of an LLC offers both flexibility and protection, making it a favored choice for authors and publishers alike. Imagine the thrill of seeing your work in print, coupled with the peace of mind that comes from knowing your personal assets are protected from potential liabilities associated with published content. This is the dual advantage of an LLC in the publishing sector. Managing publishing rights becomes more streamlined, as the LLC provides a clear framework for ownership and distribution of rights, allowing you to focus on creative endeavors without the constant worry of legal entanglements. Whether dealing with traditional print media or digital formats, an LLC helps ensure that your intellectual property remains secure, with the added benefit of potential tax efficiencies.

Revenue streams in publishing are as diverse as the stories themselves. While traditional book sales and royalties have long been the backbone of the industry, the digital age has expanded opportunities significantly. With an LLC, you can easily navigate the complexity of income from various sources. Digital content, subscriptions, and even interactive media provide new avenues for income generation. Consider the possibilities: A serialized novel released through a subscription model can reach a global audience, while digital platforms allow for targeted marketing that can increase sales exponentially. An LLC provides the structure to manage these diverse streams efficiently, ensuring that you can capitalize on every opportunity without losing focus on your creative output.

Collaboration is at the heart of many successful publishing ventures. Whether co-publishing agreements with other publishers or partnerships with authors and illustrators, these strategic alliances can expand your reach and amplify your impact. An LLC supports these collaborations by offering a flexible framework for partnership agreements. It allows you to negotiate terms that are beneficial to all parties while maintaining clear legal boundaries. By fostering such alliances, you can pool resources, share expertise, and tap into new audiences, creating a synergy that propels your publishing venture forward. The ability to form and manage these partnerships seamlessly is yet another reason why an LLC is an attractive option for those in the publishing industry.

Distribution and marketing are critical components of a successful publishing strategy. The digital revolution has transformed the landscape, offering unprecedented opportunities to reach readers directly. Utilizing online platforms for distribution enables you to bypass traditional gatekeepers and connect with your audience instantly. Whether it's through Amazon Kindle Direct Publishing or other digital storefronts, an LLC provides the infrastructure to manage sales and royalties efficiently. Targeted marketing campaigns, tailored to specific demographics or niches, become more effective with the data-driven insights that an LLC can facilitate. By leveraging these strategies, you can maximize your reach and engagement, ensuring your published works find the audience they deserve.

Case Study: Independent Publisher's Success Story

Consider the journey of an independent publisher who transitioned from a sole proprietorship to an LLC. Initially, her focus was on local authors and niche markets. However, the shift to an LLC allowed her to expand her catalog, incorporating digital formats and leveraging online distribution channels. This change not only increased her revenue streams but also provided the legal protection and credibility needed to attract higher-profile authors. By forming partnerships with illustrators and designers, she was able to offer comprehensive publishing packages, further enhancing her business's reputation. Her story illustrates how an LLC can elevate a publishing venture, providing the tools and structure necessary for sustainable growth and innovation.

7.2 Technology Startups – LLC Considerations and Strategies

In the fast-paced world of technology startups, forming an LLC can provide a solid foundation for growth and innovation. The flexibility and protection offered by an LLC make it an attractive choice for tech entrepreneurs eager to turn their vision into reality. One of the primary benefits is the ability to attract angel investors. Investors often seek assurance that their investment is protected, and an LLC's limited liability structure provides just that. It reassures investors that their personal assets are safe, encouraging them to inject capital into your startup. Furthermore, an LLC offers significant flexibility in managing equity distribution. This flexibility allows you to structure ownership in a way that aligns with your business goals and incentivizes key team members, ensuring that everyone is motivated to drive the company forward.

Protecting your intellectual property is crucial for technology startups, where innovation is the lifeblood of success. An LLC structure supports this by providing a clear framework for patent filing processes, ensuring that your groundbreaking ideas are legally protected from infringement. By securing patents, you safeguard your inventions, establishing a competitive edge in the market. Additionally, non-disclosure agreements (NDAs) are vital tools for maintaining confidentiality during collaborations and partnerships. NDAs help prevent unauthorized sharing of sensitive information, protecting your business's valuable assets. With an LLC, you can confidently engage in discussions with potential partners, investors, and collaborators, knowing that your intellectual property is safeguarded and that you have legal recourse should any breaches occur.

Scaling and expansion are often at the forefront of a tech startup's agenda, and an LLC provides the necessary framework to support this growth. Agile development methodologies, which prioritize flexibility and rapid iteration, align perfectly with the adaptable structure of an LLC. This approach allows your team to respond swiftly to market changes and customer feedback, fostering a culture of innovation and continuous improvement. Building scalable infrastructure is another critical aspect of scaling a tech startup. An LLC's structure enables you to make strategic decisions about technology investments, ensuring that your infrastructure can support increased demand as your business grows. Whether it's expanding your server capacity or enhancing your software capabilities, an LLC provides the operational flexibility needed to scale efficiently and effectively.

Regulatory compliance is a crucial consideration for tech startups, particularly in an era where data protection and privacy laws are becoming increasingly stringent. An LLC offers a robust framework for adhering to industry-specific regulations, ensuring that your business remains compliant with data protection and privacy laws. By implementing comprehensive compliance programs, you can mitigate the risk of data breaches, protecting both your business and your customers. Moreover, compliance with tech industry standards is essential for building trust and credibility with clients and partners. An LLC provides the structure to implement and maintain these standards, allowing you to focus on delivering innovative solutions without the constant worry of regulatory pitfalls. This commitment to compliance not only protects your business but also enhances your reputation in the industry, positioning you as a trusted and reliable partner in the tech ecosystem.

Case Study: From Startup to Scale-Up

Consider a tech startup that began with a small team and a big idea—a revolutionary app designed to streamline remote work collaboration. Initially formed as an LLC, the company attracted angel investors who were confident in the startup's potential, thanks to the liability protection the LLC offered. With funding secured, the team focused on scaling their infrastructure, adopting agile methodologies to iterate rapidly and respond to user feedback.

As the app gained traction, the startup navigated complex data privacy regulations, ensuring full compliance with industry standards. This commitment to innovation and compliance enabled the startup to scale successfully, eventually becoming a leader in the remote work technology space. Their journey illustrates how an LLC can provide the flexibility, protection, and stability needed to transform a startup into a thriving scale-up.

7.3 Retail and E-Commerce – Managing an LLC

Operating a retail or e-commerce business within an LLC structure provides distinct advantages, especially in the dynamic and often unpredictable world of commerce. One of the primary benefits is the limited liability protection it offers against product-related claims. Picture a scenario where a product defect leads to a customer lawsuit. As an LLC, your personal assets remain shielded from business liabilities, offering peace of mind that your home or personal savings are not at risk. This separation is crucial for entrepreneurs who want to innovate and push boundaries without the constant fear of personal financial devastation. Furthermore, an LLC enhances flexibility in managing inventory, allowing for strategic decisions that can adapt to market demand. Whether you're dealing with seasonal products or rapid shifts in consumer preferences, the LLC's structure supports agile inventory management, enabling you to respond swiftly to changes without the red tape that might encumber corporations.

Inventory and supply chain management are critical to the success of any retail or e-commerce operation. Implementing a just-in-time inventory system can significantly optimize your processes, reducing waste and lowering storage costs. Just-in-time systems ensure that inventory is ordered and received only as needed, aligning supply closely with demand. This approach minimizes excess stock and frees up capital, allowing you to invest in other areas of your business. Additionally, effective supplier relationship management is vital. Building strong partnerships with reliable suppliers ensures a steady flow of products and can lead to favorable terms and discounts. Regular communication and negotiation can solidify these relationships, providing a competitive edge in the market. By prioritizing these strategies, your LLC can maintain a lean, efficient operation that maximizes profitability and minimizes risk.

In the digital age, leveraging e-commerce platforms is not just an option— it's a necessity for growth. These platforms offer unparalleled opportunities to reach a global audience and increase sales. To make the most of these opportunities, focus on optimizing your online store with effective SEO strategies. Search engine optimization ensures that your products are visible to potential customers, driving organic traffic to your site. Keywords, meta descriptions, and quality content all play a role in improving your search engine rankings, making it easier for customers to find your products. Once visitors arrive, exceptional customer service becomes the differentiator. Implementing best practices, such as responsive communication and personalized support, enhances the shopping experience, building customer trust and loyalty. An LLC's flexible management structure allows you to implement these strategies seamlessly, adapting to customer needs with agility.

Marketing and customer engagement are the lifeblood of any successful retail or e-commerce business. Building brand loyalty is paramount, and one effective way to achieve this is through loyalty programs. These programs reward repeat customers, encouraging continued patronage and increasing lifetime customer value. Whether it's through points systems, exclusive discounts, or special offers, loyalty programs create a sense of belonging and appreciation among your customer base. Additionally, social media marketing campaigns provide a powerful platform to engage with consumers directly. By creating compelling content and fostering interactive dialogue, you can cultivate a community around your brand. Social media allows your LLC to reach potential customers where they spend a significant portion of their time, increasing visibility and driving sales. With the right blend of marketing strategies, your LLC can build a strong, loyal customer base that supports sustained growth and success.

Resource List: E-Commerce Tools and Platforms

Consider exploring these tools and platforms to enhance your e-commerce operations:

- Shopify: An all-in-one e-commerce platform for building and managing online stores.
- WooCommerce: A customizable plugin for WordPress, ideal for integrating e-commerce into existing websites.
- HubSpot CRM: A customer relationship management tool that supports sales, marketing, and customer service activities.
- Google Analytics: Provides insights into website traffic and customer behavior, informing data-driven decisions.

By leveraging these resources, you can streamline your e-commerce operations, enhance customer engagement, and drive business growth effectively.

7.4 Professional Services – Optimizing Your LLC Structure

In the realm of professional services, the umbrella of an LLC offers a multitude of benefits that can safeguard your practice and enhance your reputation. Whether you're offering legal advice, financial consulting, or any specialized service, the protection an LLC affords cannot be overstated. It acts as a barrier between your personal and business liabilities, ensuring that your personal assets remain untouched should any legal disputes arise. Clients tend to trust businesses that operate under an LLC because it reflects a commitment to professionalism and accountability. This trust is crucial in building long-term relationships, as clients are more inclined to engage with service providers who demonstrate stability and dedication to their craft.

Pricing strategies in professional services require careful consideration and strategic planning. In an industry where your expertise is your product, setting the right price is crucial to attracting and retaining clients. One effective approach is value-based pricing, where fees are aligned with the perceived value of your services. This model allows you to charge more for services that offer significant client benefits, reflecting the quality and impact of your work. Retainer agreements are another effective strategy, providing a steady income stream while fostering client loyalty. By offering packages at a fixed monthly rate, you ensure consistent revenue while giving clients the assurance of ongoing support. This model not only stabilizes your income but also cements your role as a trusted advisor within your client's business framework.

Maintaining strong client relationships is at the heart of any successful service-based business. Effective communication is the cornerstone of these relationships, ensuring that expectations are met and trust is maintained. Regular check-ins, updates on project progress, and open lines of communication help build rapport and demonstrate your commitment to client satisfaction. Encouraging feedback is equally important, providing valuable insights into areas for improvement. Implementing a structured feedback process not only enhances your service quality but also reinforces your dedication to client satisfaction. By addressing concerns promptly and adapting to client needs, you solidify your reputation as a responsive and reliable service provider.

Navigating industry-specific compliance requirements is another critical aspect of managing a professional services LLC. Depending on your field, you may need to meet specific licensing and certification standards. These requirements ensure that your practice adheres to industry norms and regulations, protecting both your business and your clients. It's essential to stay informed about changes in these standards, as non-compliance can lead to significant legal and financial repercussions. Adhering to professional standards not only safeguards your practice but also enhances your credibility, reassuring clients of your expertise and commitment to ethical practices.

7.5 Hospitality and Food Services – Unique LLC Challenges

Imagine the bustling atmosphere of a restaurant, the clinking of glasses, and the aroma of dishes wafting through the air. In the hospitality and food services industry, delivering exceptional guest experiences is paramount. However, with great service comes great responsibility, particularly in managing liability. An LLC can offer a safety net, ensuring that your personal assets remain untouchable in the face of legal claims. Whether it's a slip-and-fall incident or a dispute over a meal, the LLC structure provides a buffer, protecting your personal wealth from business liabilities. This protection allows you to focus on creating memorable experiences for your guests without the constant fear of personal financial risk.

The flexibility of an LLC is invaluable in hospitality, where menu and service offerings must adapt to changing consumer tastes and seasonal availability. Whether you're revamping your menu to incorporate local ingredients or launching a new service, such as delivery or catering, an LLC allows you to pivot swiftly. This adaptability is crucial for staying competitive in an ever-evolving market. The ability to make quick, strategic changes without the constraints of cumbersome corporate protocols ensures that your business remains relevant and responsive to customer demands. This flexibility extends beyond offerings to encompass staffing and resource allocation, allowing you to make decisions that align with your business goals.

Operational efficiency is the backbone of any successful food service establishment. Implementing robust inventory management systems can significantly reduce waste and optimize resource allocation. These systems provide real-time insights into stock levels, enabling you to make informed purchasing decisions that minimize spoilage and maximize profitability. Efficient staff scheduling and management are equally important. By employing scheduling software, you can ensure optimal coverage during peak hours while avoiding unnecessary labor costs during slower periods. This not only enhances productivity but also boosts staff morale by providing predictable work hours and reducing burnout.

Compliance with health and safety regulations is non-negotiable in the food services industry. Securing food safety certifications is a vital step in demonstrating your commitment to quality and safety. These certifications not only protect your customers but also enhance your reputation, instilling confidence in your brand. Regular health inspections are another critical component of compliance. By maintaining a clean and safe environment, you not only meet regulatory requirements but also create a pleasant dining experience for your guests. This commitment to excellence sets your establishment apart, building trust and loyalty among your clientele.

Customer satisfaction is the ultimate measure of success in hospitality. Implementing customer feedback systems allows you to gather valuable insights into guest experiences, identifying areas for improvement and celebrating successes. Whether through comment cards, online surveys, or social media interactions, listening to your customers is key to delivering personalized service. Tailoring experiences to individual preferences not only enhances satisfaction but also fosters loyalty, turning one-time visitors into repeat patrons. Personalization can be as simple as remembering a regular's favorite dish or offering customized recommendations, creating a sense of connection and care that resonates with guests.

Effective marketing strategies are essential for attracting and retaining customers in a competitive landscape. Highlighting your unique selling points, such as a signature dish or an eco-friendly initiative, can differentiate your brand and draw in curious diners. Collaborating with local businesses can also amplify your reach. Whether it's partnering with a local brewery for a themed event or sourcing ingredients from nearby farms, these alliances can enhance your brand's appeal and strengthen community ties. By leveraging these strategies, you can create a buzz around your establishment, driving foot traffic and boosting sales.

In the hospitality industry, the intersection of protection, flexibility, and service is where success thrives. An LLC provides the framework to navigate these challenges, ensuring that your focus remains on delivering exceptional experiences. As you continue to explore the potential of an LLC for your business, remember that the right structure can make all the difference in achieving sustainable growth and lasting impact.

I hope in these business examples, you see some of your own scenarios. You can claim all the same deductions and expenses trading as a sole trader, the same as you can as an LLC, so there's no benefit there. You do get tax savings in an LLC by paying at personal income tax rates rather than company tax rates. The main benefits of an LLC are the asset protection and the fact that you have peace of mind knowing that if you are sued in our ever increasingly litigious country, your liability is limited to the company only and not your personal assets. And secondly, it's the perception from the people that interact with your business, whether it's your own staff, customers, or investors, that as an LLC, you mean business and take your business seriously.

Chapter 8

Enhancing Your LLC Journey

Picture this: You're at a crossroads, where the paths of knowledge and opportunity converge. You're not just running an LLC; you're steering it toward a future filled with potential. As a business person, sole trader, freelancer, or publisher, you're always on the lookout for ways to elevate your game. This chapter is your guide to a treasure trove of resources that can shape your entrepreneurial voyage. It's about embracing learning opportunities that fit into your busy schedule, offering insights that are both practical and transformative.

In the realm of self-paced learning, the digital age has bestowed upon us a plethora of resources. Online courses on business management stand as pillars of knowledge, accessible at the click of a button. They allow you to delve into subjects like strategic planning or financial management at your own pace. Websites like LLC University® offer free courses covering everything from LLC basics to intricate tax details. These resources provide step-by-step guidance, ensuring that you can learn without the pressure of traditional classroom settings. Webinars hosted by industry experts are another goldmine. They bring the wisdom of seasoned professionals right to your screen, offering real-time insights and the chance to ask questions directly.

Books have long been the silent mentors of many a successful entrepreneur. "The E-Myth Revisited" by Michael E. Gerber is one such classic that dissects the common pitfalls in business management and offers strategies to over-come them. Meanwhile, "Built to Last" by Jim Collins explores the enduring qualities of successful companies, providing a blueprint for sustainability and growth. These readings offer deep dives into the philosophy of business, challenging you to think beyond the day-to-day and consider the legacy you want to build. They are companions that can sit on your nightstand, waiting to offer guidance when you need it most.

Interactive workshops and seminars add another layer of learning, one that is tactile and immediate. Local business seminars offer the chance to network with peers while gaining insights into regional market dynamics. These events are often rich with case studies and real-world applications that resonate with your own experiences. Industry-specific workshops can be particularly beneficial, providing targeted knowledge that addresses the unique challenges of your sector. By participating in these events, you place yourself in a learning environment that is both vibrant and practical, allowing you to absorb knowledge through direct engagement and interaction with others.

Mentorship programs are a beacon of guidance, illuminating the path with the light of accumulated experience. Engaging with a mentor can accelerate your growth by providing insights tailored to your personal journey. Mentors offer more than advice; they provide accountability, constructive feedback, and a broader network. Finding the right mentor involves identifying your specific needs and seeking individuals whose experience aligns with your goals. Once you establish this connection, a structured mentorship program can amplify the benefits. Whether through regular meetings or casual check-ins, this relationship fosters a dynamic exchange of ideas and strategies that can propel you toward success.

Reflection Section: Personal Learning Plan

Take a moment to reflect on your current learning habits. Consider what areas of your business knowledge could be expanded or refined. List three learning resources you plan to explore in the next month, such as an online course, a book, and a local seminar. Note any specific skills or insights you hope to gain from each. This exercise is designed to help you create a personal learning plan that aligns with your business aspirations, ensuring that you continue to grow alongside your LLC.

8.1 Building a Supportive Community of LLC Owners

Imagine walking into a room buzzing with enthusiasm, where every conversation sparks a new idea or opportunity. This is the power of networking. As a business owner, the connections you make can be invaluable. Attending local business meetups allows you to engage with others in your field, learn from their experiences, and even find potential collaborators. These gatherings aren't just about exchanging business cards; they're about building relationships that can lead to future partnerships or even friendships. Joining professional associations offers similar benefits on a broader scale. These organizations provide a platform to meet industry leaders and stay informed about the latest trends and challenges. They can also offer resources and support that are specific to your business needs, giving you a competitive edge.

Forming mastermind groups takes networking to a more intimate level. These small groups consist of like-minded individuals who meet regularly to discuss their goals and challenges. Accountability sessions are a key component, where each member shares their progress and receives feedback. This peer-to-peer support system is incredibly effective, as it combines diverse perspectives with a shared commitment to growth. Members share resources and advice, offering solutions that you might not have considered on your own. This collaborative approach not only helps in overcoming business obstacles but also fosters a sense of camaraderie. Knowing you have a group of people who understand your struggles and are invested in your success can be a powerful motivator.

In today's digital age, online forums offer another avenue for connecting with fellow LLC owners. Platforms such as Reddit have communities focused on entrepreneurship, where users exchange advice and share their experiences. Participating in these discussions can provide you with insights that are both broad and specific, tailored to the concerns of business owners like yourself. LinkedIn groups are another excellent resource for professional development and networking. By engaging in these spaces, you can expand your network beyond geographical limitations and tap into a wealth of information from around the world. Online communities also provide the flexibility to interact at your convenience, making them an accessible resource at any stage of your business.

Networking and community-building often lead to collaborative opportunities that can significantly enhance your business. Joint ventures and partnerships arise naturally when you connect with individuals who share your vision or complement your skill set. For example, co-hosting events with partners can double your audience reach and create a buzz that benefits all involved. Similarly, cross-promotional marketing efforts can introduce your business to new markets and demographics. These collaborations not only amplify your marketing efforts but also distribute the workload, making ambitious projects more manageable. The key is to approach partnerships with an open mind and a clear understanding of mutual goals. By fostering a cooperative spirit, you can create synergies that propel your business forward.

Resource List: Networking Platforms for LLC Owners

- Meetup.com: Find local business meetups and networking events tailored to your industry.
- LinkedIn Groups: Join professional groups for business development and industry-specific discussions.
- Reddit: Engage in entrepreneurial communities for advice and shared experiences.
- Professional Associations: Explore organizations related to your field for resources and networking opportunities.

8.2 Utilizing Online Tools and Platforms for LLC Management

In today's increasingly digital landscape, managing an LLC efficiently often hinges on the effective use of online tools and platforms. These resources streamline operations, enhance productivity, and foster collaboration in ways that were unimaginable just a few decades ago. For those at the helm of an LLC, project management software can be a game-changer. Consider Asana, a robust tool designed to help you keep track of tasks and deadlines with ease. It allows you to assign tasks, set due dates, and monitor progress, ensuring that everyone on your team is aligned and informed. With its intuitive interface, Asana makes juggling multiple projects a less daunting task. Then there's Trello, known for its visual approach to project management. Utilizing boards and cards, Trello provides a clear, visual snapshot of your project's status. It's especially useful for teams that benefit from seeing workflows laid out in a dynamic, engaging format. Both tools support collaboration, making it easier to coordinate efforts and communicate effectively, even across distances.

Financial oversight is another crucial area where technology can make a significant impact. Enter Xero, an accounting platform that simplifies the often-complex world of business finances. With Xero, you can manage invoices, track expenses, and even reconcile bank transactions, all from a single interface. It integrates smoothly with other financial tools, giving you a comprehensive view of your financial health. Alongside Xero, consider Expensify for tracking expenses. This app allows users to scan receipts and manage expenses effortlessly. It's particularly beneficial for businesses that deal with frequent travel or client meetings, as it reduces the hassle of manual data entry and ensures accuracy in expense reporting. Together, these platforms help you maintain financial clarity and reduce the likelihood of errors, which can be costly and time-consuming to correct.

Communication is the backbone of any successful team, especially in an era where remote work is becoming the norm. Tools like Slack revolutionize team messaging, providing channels for specific projects or topics, thus minimizing email overload and enhancing real-time communication. Slack's integration capabilities mean you can connect it with other apps your team already uses, creating a streamlined workflow. You can also use Microsoft Teams chat feature, which integrates with the Microsoft suite of tools and stores files in a shared space for all to access. I personally prefer this to Google's workspace option. For video conferencing, Zoom stands out as a reliable option. It offers clear audio and video quality and is equipped with features like screen sharing and breakout rooms, making it ideal for team meetings, client presentations, or even virtual networking events. These tools ensure that distance doesn't hinder collaboration and that your team remains cohesive and productive, regardless of physical location.

Managing customer relationships effectively is crucial for sustaining and growing your business. HubSpot CRM is a powerful tool for sales management, allowing you to track interactions, manage leads, and automate sales processes. Its user-friendly dashboard provides insights into customer behaviors and preferences, enabling you to tailor your approach and improve customer satisfaction. Similarly, Mailchimp is a valuable asset for email marketing. It helps you design compelling emails, segment your audience, and analyze the performance of your campaigns. By leveraging Mailchimp, you can maintain regular contact with your customers, keeping them informed and engaged with your brand. These platforms not only enhance customer interaction but also provide the data necessary to refine your strategies and optimize your marketing efforts.

By incorporating these online tools and platforms into your LLC's operations, you position your business to thrive in a competitive marketplace. They offer the efficiency, accuracy, and connectivity that modern businesses require, freeing up time and resources to focus on strategic growth and innovation.

8.3 Continuous Learning and Adaptation for Business Growth

In the ever-evolving landscape of entrepreneurship, fostering a culture of continuous improvement is not just beneficial—it's imperative. Encouraging ongoing development within your team and yourself can lead to innovation that keeps your business competitive. One way to nurture this mindset is by implementing feedback loops. These loops involve a structured process where feedback is regularly sought from employees, clients, and other stakeholders, then analyzed and acted upon. This not only enhances the quality of your offerings but also promotes a sense of ownership and involvement among your team, as they see their input directly influencing the business trajectory.

Regular skills assessments are another critical component of cultivating continuous improvement. By periodically evaluating the skills and competencies of your team, you can identify gaps and opportunities for development. This process ensures that your team remains equipped to tackle new challenges and adapt to industry changes. It also empowers employees by aligning their personal growth with the company's goals, fostering a more engaged and motivated workforce. Skills assessments can be informal, such as regular one-on-one meetings, or more structured, like annual reviews with specific metrics and objectives.

Staying informed about industry trends and developments is essential for maintaining a competitive edge. Subscribing to industry newsletters provides a steady stream of information about the latest innovations, market shifts, and regulatory changes. This knowledge enables you to anticipate trends and adjust your strategies accordingly. Virtual conferences have also become a valuable resource, offering access to a wealth of expertise without the need for travel. These events often feature keynotes from industry leaders and panels that explore emerging trends, providing insights that can inform your strategic planning and decision-making processes.

Adopting agile methodologies can significantly enhance your business's adaptability. The Scrum framework, for example, breaks projects into smaller, manageable iterations called sprints, allowing for regular reassessment and adjustment. This iterative approach ensures that your team can respond quickly to changes and challenges, rather than being locked into a rigid plan. The Kanban method complements this by providing a visual workflow that helps manage tasks efficiently, ensuring that resources are allocated optimally and bottlenecks are addressed promptly. Together, these agile practices foster a culture of flexibility and responsiveness, crucial traits in today's fast-paced business environment.

Encouraging experimentation and innovation within your organization can drive growth and uncover new opportunities. Pilot programs for new products or services allow you to test concepts on a small scale before committing significant resources. This approach minimizes risk while providing valuable insights into customer reactions and market potential. Similarly, establishing innovation labs within your business can create a dedicated space for developing and testing new ideas. These labs encourage creative thinking and collaboration, often leading to breakthroughs that can set your business apart from competitors. By fostering an environment where experimentation is valued and supported, you create a culture that is not only resilient in the face of change but also proactive in seeking out new avenues for growth.

8.4 Planning for Long-Term Business Sustainability

When considering the future of your LLC, it's crucial to focus on sustainability. This isn't just about environmental efforts, though that's a vital part. Sustainability encompasses how your business can thrive for decades to come. Developing a sustainability strategy means looking at your operations through a lens of longevity and impact. Implementing environmental practices not only helps the planet but also reduces costs. Think about energy-efficient technologies that cut down utility bills and lower your carbon footprint. Consider utilizing renewable energy sources or recycling programs that not only appeal to eco-conscious consumers but also set a standard within your industry.

Social responsibility should be at the core of your strategy. It's about aligning your business practices with ethical standards and community values. Initiatives like fair labor practices, supporting local charities, or engaging in community development projects can build a positive reputation and foster customer loyalty. Consumers today are looking for businesses that reflect their values, and being socially responsible can differentiate your brand in a crowded market. By integrating these initiatives into your business model, you create a culture that values both profit and purpose, which resonates with customers and employees alike.

Financial sustainability is equally vital. It's not enough to have a profitable quarter; you need to ensure your business can weather economic storms. Diversifying revenue streams can protect your business from market fluctuations or seasonal downturns. Explore new markets or develop complementary products that align with your existing offerings. Building strong cash reserves acts as a safety net for unforeseen challenges. This might mean setting aside a percentage of profits each month or reinvesting in cost-saving technologies. Financial resilience allows your business to adapt and thrive, regardless of external pressures.

Technology plays a pivotal role in creating sustainable business practices. Digital transformation can streamline operations, reduce waste, and improve efficiency. Consider adopting cloud-based systems that enhance collaboration and decrease reliance on paper. Energy-efficient equipment and smart technology can drastically cut down operational costs and environmental impact. By staying abreast of technological advancements, your business can operate more efficiently and sustainably, setting a benchmark for others to follow. Technology isn't just a tool; it's a vital ally in your quest for sustainability.

Finally, planning for the future means thinking about leadership transitions. Succession planning ensures that your business continues to thrive even when there's a change at the top. Identify potential successors early and invest in their development. This might involve leadership programs or mentorship opportunities that prepare them for future roles. Cultivating internal talent ensures continuity and preserves the values and vision of your business. A well-executed succession plan can prevent disruptions and maintain the confidence of clients and employees. It's about building a legacy that outlasts any single leader.

8.5 Inspiring Stories from Successful LLC Entrepreneurs

Consider the tale of a tech startup that began in a modest garage, a familiar setting for many innovative companies. This particular venture focused on developing cutting-edge software solutions aimed at revolutionizing the way we interact with digital devices. Despite the initial hurdles of securing funding and fine-tuning their product, the founders persevered. They leveraged their LLC structure to attract investors who were assured by the personal liability protection it provided. This setup also allowed them the flexibility to reinvest profits directly into research and development. Fast forward a few years, and the company now scales globally, with operations in multiple countries and a diverse team driving continuous innovation. Their story serves as a testament to the power of strategic planning and the importance of staying adaptable in a fast-paced industry.

On the other hand, a creative agency offers a different perspective on success. Founded by a group of passionate designers and marketers, this LLC set out to redefine client experiences through innovative digital campaigns. Initially, they struggled with finding their niche in a crowded market. However, by focusing on the unique strengths of their team and embracing a culture of creativity, they were able to carve out a distinct identity. They utilized digital marketing strategies to reach new audiences, rapidly growing their client base. Building a strong brand identity became their hallmark, with each project showcasing their distinct style and commitment to excellence. Today, they are known for their ability to transform ordinary campaigns into extraordinary experiences, leaving a lasting impression on both clients and audiences alike.

The lessons learned from these entrepreneurs are invaluable. Overcoming initial challenges often requires a blend of perseverance and flexibility. It's about recognizing that setbacks are part of the process and that every obstacle presents an opportunity for growth. Cultivating innovation and creativity is another key takeaway. Whether through regular brainstorming sessions or fostering an environment where new ideas are encouraged, nurturing creativity can lead to groundbreaking solutions and strategies. These entrepreneurs also highlight the importance of digital marketing, leveraging online platforms to connect with broader audiences and drive growth. By understanding the nuances of their target demographics, they crafted campaigns that resonated deeply, ultimately leading to increased brand loyalty and recognition.

Reflecting on these stories, it's clear that the strategies implemented by successful LLCs are both practical and inspirational. They encourage you to take stock of your own business practices and identify areas ripe for improvement. What processes can be streamlined? Where can you inject more creativity? Setting ambitious yet achievable goals is crucial. By establishing clear objectives and mapping out a path to reach them, you create a road map for success. These stories remind you that while the path to success may be fraught with challenges, it is also filled with opportunities to learn and grow. Each step taken is a chance to refine your approach and move closer to your vision.

Don't move on to the next chapter without doing the following;

1. Does further learning to grow your knowledge and business acumen resonate with you? Do you need to do research on what/who that could be?
2. Do you have a vision for how you want to handle sustainability in your business? How can you implement this from the beginning and communicate it across your platforms?

Conclusion

As we reach the end of our journey together, I want to take a moment to reflect on the purpose of this book. When I set out to write "LLC for Beginners Made Easy," my goal was simple: to demystify the process of setting up and managing an LLC. Drawing from my own experiences as a CPA and the lessons I've learned along the way, I aimed to provide you with a clear, step-by-step guide that would empower you to take control of your entrepreneurial future.

Throughout these pages, we've covered a wide range of topics essential to understanding and navigating the world of LLCs. From the basics of what an LLC is and how it differs from other business structures to the nitty-gritty details of tax implications and compliance requirements, we've left no stone unturned. We've explored the benefits of forming an LLC, such as personal asset protection and enhanced credibility, and we've delved into the practical steps involved in setting one up, like choosing a business name and filing Articles of Organization.

But this book is about more than just the technical aspects of LLCs. It's about equipping you with the knowledge and confidence to make informed decisions for your business. It's about providing you with real-life examples and case studies that illustrate the power of the LLC structure in action. And it's about offering you a road map for success, complete with strategies for growth, management tips, and resources for continuous learning.

As you reflect on the key takeaways from this book, I hope you'll remember that forming an LLC is not just about paperwork and legal formalities. It's about taking a proactive step towards protecting your personal assets, optimizing your tax strategy, and creating a solid foundation for your business to thrive. It's about embracing the flexibility and adaptability that an LLC offers, allowing you to pivot and grow as your business evolves.

But the journey doesn't end here. Armed with the knowledge and tools provided in this book, it's time for you to take action. Whether you're a freelancer ready to take your business to the next level, a small business owner looking to minimize risk, or an entrepreneur with a groundbreaking idea, the LLC structure can help you achieve your goals. So, take that first step. Consult with a trusted professional, gather your documents, and embark on the process of forming your LLC.

As you navigate the exciting world of entrepreneurship, remember that you're not alone. The stories and examples shared in this book are a testament to the countless individuals who have successfully leveraged the LLC structure to build thriving businesses. From tech startups to creative agencies, from e-commerce ventures to professional services, LLCs have provided a solid foundation for entrepreneurs across industries.

The path ahead may not always be easy, but with the right knowledge and mindset, the possibilities are endless. As you apply the lessons learned from this book, stay curious, stay adaptable, and stay committed to your vision. Embrace the challenges as opportunities for growth, and celebrate the milestones along the way.

I want to thank you for joining me on this journey of learning and discovery. Your dedication to understanding the intricacies of LLCs and your commitment to improving your business outcomes are truly admirable. I hope that this book has not only provided you with practical guidance but also inspired you to dream big and take bold action.

As you close this book and step into your entrepreneurial future, know that you have the tools and the knowledge to succeed. The LLC structure is a powerful ally in your journey, offering protection, flexibility, and opportunity. Embrace it, leverage it, and watch your business soar.

Here's to your success and to the incredible journey ahead.

With gratitude,
Emma

References

- *Pros and Cons of a Limited Liability Company (LLC)* https://www.investoped ia.com/articles/investing/091014/basics-forming-limited-liability-com pany-llc.asp
- *LLC vs. S Corp: What's the Difference? – Investopedia* https://www.investope dia.com/articles/personal-finance/011216/s-corp-vs-llc-which-should- i-choose.asp#:~:text=An%20LLC%20offers%20a%20more,corporation %20is%20a%20tax%20classification.
- *7 Common LLC Myths You Need To Know* https://www.zenbusiness.com/llc -myths/
- *7 Well-Known LLC Examples from Popular Companies* https://www.doola.co m/blog/llc-examples/
- *How to Start an LLC: Complete Guide* https://www.wolterskluwer.com/en/e xpert-insights/how-to-form-an-llc-what-is-an-llc-advantages-disad vantages-and-more
- *How to Choose an LLC Name: Tips for Naming Your LLC* https://www.legalzo om.com/articles/how-to-choose-an-llc-name
- *LLC Requirements by State: Everything You Need to Know* https://www.upco unsel.com/llc-requirements-by-state
- *What is an operating agreement? Do I need one for my LLC?* https://legal.tho msonreuters.com/en/insights/articles/what-is-an-operating-agreemen t#:~:text=The%20major%20pros%20of%20an,adapted%20to%20a%20 specific%20LLC.
- *LLC pass-through taxation: What small business owners need …* https://www. wolterskluwer.com/en/expert-insights/llc-pass-through-taxation-wha t-small-business-owners-need-to-know#:~:text=The%20main%20be

nefit%20of%20pass,are%20subject%20to%20double%20taxation.

- *Best Accounting Software for Small Businesses of 2025* https://www.nerdwal let.com/p/best/small-business/accounting-software
- *14 Tax Write-Offs for LLC* https://www.freshbooks.com/hub/taxes/tax-wri te-offs-for-llc?srsltid=AfmBOoqhDwwepoRnjebz5qUVbeZwuLTdYE89m ZmKszuCeW-NR_aI4ZAl
- *State Guide to LLC Report and Tax Filing Requirements* https://www.nolo.co m/legal-encyclopedia/50-state-guide-annual-report-tax-filing-requir ements-llcs
- *Annual Report Requirements by Entity Type* https://www.harborcompliance. com/llc-corporation-annual-report
- *Compliance and governance for corporations and LLCs …* https://www.wolter skluwer.com/en/expert-insights/compliance-and-governance-for-corp orations-and-llcs-under-state-business-entity-laws
- *7 Common Legal Pitfalls Small Business Owners Must …* https://www.linkedi n.com/pulse/7-common-legal-pitfalls-small-business-owners-must-a void-woods-409gc
- *An Update on the State Tax Treatment of LLCs and LLPs* https://www.taxnot es.com/lr/resolve/special-reports/an-update-on-the-state-tax-treatm ent-of-llcs-and-llps/7lmbl
- *Strategies to Successfully Grow Your LLC* https://www.startmotionmedia.co m/strategiesonhowtosuccessfullygrowyourllcbu/
- *Financing Options for Small Businesses* https://www.nerdwallet.com/article /small-business/small-business-financing
- *Can LLCs Hire Employees? An Essential Guide* https://www.hrfuture.net/tal ent-management/hiring/can-llcs-hire-employees-an-essential-guide/
- *How Technology is Revolutionizing Business Operations* https://www.troop messenger.com/blogs/revolutionizing-business-operations#:~:text=Ad opting%20digital%20tools%20and%20software,and%20effectively%20 a%20company%20runs.
- *LLC to S-Corp: Step-by-Step Guide* https://www.simplifyllc.com/llc-glossa ry/how-to-change-llc-to-s-corp/
- *How to Protect Your Personal Assets as an LLC Owner* https://www.legalzoo

m.com/articles/llc-asset-protection-how-to-protect-your-personal-assets-as-an-llc-owner

- *Advanced Tax Strategies for LLCs and Partnerships* https://www.wiley.com/en-us/Advanced+Tax+Strategies+for+LLCs+and+Partnerships-p-9781119748731
- *The Ultimate Guide to Multi-Member LLC Operating ...* https://www.legalgps.com/llc-operating-agreement/blog/the-ultimate-guide-to-multi-member-llc-operating-agreements
- *Should I Start an LLC As a Freelancer?* https://www.keepertax.com/posts/should-i-start-an-llc-as-a-freelancer
- *Should Authors Set Up an LLC? Pros, Cons, and Why It ...* https://www.storyflowsolutions.com/blog/llc-for-authors-pros-and-cons
- *The Ultimate Guide to Forming an LLC for Startup Success* https://www.marshmallowchallenge.com/blog/the-ultimate-guide-to-forming-an-llc-for-startup-success/
- *Retail E-Commerce for Your Business: Trends, Best ...* https://resources.purolator.com/retail-e-commerce-best-practices-and-strategies/
- *Free LLC Classes and Online Courses* https://www.llcuniversity.com/learning-center/
- *Mentoring Entrepreneurs: Benefits, Best Practices, and More* https://www.mentoringcomplete.com/role-of-mentorship-in-entrepreneurial-success/
- *The best project management software for small businesses* https://zapier.com/blog/best-project-management-software-small-business/
- *Startup Success Stories: How LLCs Paved the Way ...* https://personalbrandingblog.com/startup-success-stories-how-llcs-paved-the-way-for-unicorns/

About the Author

Also by Emma Maxwell

www.ingramcontent.com/pod-product-compliance
Lightning Source LLC
Chambersburg PA
CBHW071716210326
41597CB00017B/2505